ANTONY AND ~

Kenneth Muir was an internationally renowned Shakespeare scholar. He was editor of *Shakespeare Survey* between 1965 and 1980, a Vice-President of the International Shakespeare Association and Professor Emeritus in English Literature at the University of Liverpool. He prepared numerous critical editions of the works of major poets and dramatists as well as being the author of many critical works, including *Shakespeare's Tragic Sequence*. He translated sixteen French and Spanish plays, and had considerable experience as an amateur actor and producer: he directed one production of *King Lear* and years later played Gloucester in another. Kenneth Muir died in 1996.

Penguin Critical Studies
Advisory Editors:
Stephen Coote and Bryan Loughrey

William Shakespeare

Antony and Cleopatra

Kenneth Muir

Penguin Books

PENGUIN BOOKS

Published by the Penguin Group
Penguin Books Ltd, 27 Wrights Lane, London W8 5TZ, England
Penguin Putnam Inc., 375 Hudson Street, New York, New York 10014, USA
Penguin Books Australia Ltd, Ringwood, Victoria, Australia
Penguin Books Canada Ltd, 10 Alcorn Avenue, Toronto, Ontario, Canada M4V 3B2
Penguin Books India (P) Ltd, 11, Community Centre, Panchsheel Park,
New Delhi – 110 017, India
Penguin Books (NZ) Ltd, Private Bag 102902, NSMC, Auckland, New Zealand
Penguin Books (South Africa) (Pty) Ltd, 5 Watkins Street, Denver Ext 4,
Johannesburg 2094, South Africa

Penguin Books Ltd, Registered Offices: Harmondsworth, Middlesex, England

First published in Penguin Masterstudies 1987
Reprinted in Critical Studies 1988
2

Printed in England by Clays Ltd, St Ives plc

Contents

Preface

This book is geared to Emrys Jones's admirable edition of the play (Penguin Books, 1977). Quotations are in the text he provides, But as all modern editions of *Antony and Cleopatra* are derived from the text published in 1623, seven years after Shakespeare's death, their actual texts differ little: where they do differ is in their notes and interpretations. Among the editions I have consulted are those of M. R. Ridley (Arden) and J. Dover Wilson (Cambridge).

It will be seen that there are chapters on the sources used by Shakespeare, on the construction of the play (often misunderstood because of its unauthorized division into five acts), on Shakespeare's method of characterization, on different interpretations of the play, a scene-by-scene commentary, and a note on the historical background, supplied with a map to enable the reader to follow the action from one part of the Roman world to another. There is, finally, a list of books for further reading that may be used to qualify statements made in earlier chapters and to enable readers to follow up points in which they are specially interested.

The chapters are interrelated. Although, for example, the main characters are discussed in Chapter 3, they are also discussed from different angles in other chapters and in the Commentary. To take one example out of many, Enobarbus's desertion is discussed in the commentary on Act IV (p. 97), in the chapter on construction (p. 32) and in the chapter on characterization (p. 39); but it is to be hoped that these different discussions will prevent the perpetration of those neat and misleading character sketches which adorned many editions and which examiners were unfairly thought to favour. There is, inevitably, a certain amount of duplication, but the compensating advantages are obvious.

Any writer on Shakespeare is indebted to scores of previous critics, and the list for further reading is an acknowledgement of my most obvious debts. Less obvious ones are to colleagues and friends during the last fifty years, from Sean O'Loughlin in the thirties, Wilson Knight and Arnold Kettle in the forties, Ernest Schanzer, George Hunter and Inga-Stina Ewbank in the fifties and sixties, and Ann Thompson and Philip Edwards thereafter. To all my thanks.

Kenneth Muir

1. Sources

The main source of *Antony and Cleopatra* was Plutarch's *Life of Marcus Antonius* in Sir Thomas North's translation (from Jacques Amyot's French version of the Greek original), which Shakespeare had already used for *Julius Caesar* some nine years previously. Indeed, his acquaintance with Plutarch's *Lives* goes back earlier than that, since he used the *Life of Theseus*, the first of the collection, for some details in *A Midsummer Night's Dream*. He must have learnt of Cleopatra's spectacular suicide at school, where even those who had what Ben Jonson called 'small Latin' would read some of Horace's poems. One ode, '*Nunc est bibendum*' ('Now's the Time for Drinking') celebrates the defeat of Egypt, but ends with admiration for Cleopatra's honourable exit.[1] Soon afterwards, we may suppose, Shakespeare read *The Legend of Good Women* in which Chaucer included Cleopatra in his celebration of Love's martyrs. Not all writers were so sympathetic. In the first instalment of *The Faerie Queene* (1590), Spenser condemned the lovers for their 'wastful Pride and wanton Riotise' (I.iv.46); and in the second instalment of the poem (1596), Antony was condemned as a slave of passion:

> And so did warlike *Antony* neglect
> The worlds whole rule for Cleopatras sight.
> Such wondrous powre hath wemens fair aspect
> To captive men (V.viii.2)

Montaigne, another of Shakespeare's favourite writers, was equally condemnatory of Antony. This, indeed, was the common attitude of moralists, historians and preachers, among whom we may include many of Shakespeare's critics. But when Shakespeare began his play, he must have been struck by Plutarch's ambivalent attitude. On the one hand, Antony was ruined by his infatuation; on the other, Cleopatra was bewitchingly attractive, and as the Ptolemies were of Greek origin, Plutarch may have derived some secret satisfaction that his fellow-countrywoman had overreached Caesar.

The portraits of Antony and Cleopatra in the play are in essentials based on Plutarch's. The character of Antony in *Julius Caesar* is determined partly by the fact that the conspirators are the central characters, and we look at him, as a playboy, through their eyes. Plutarch provided evidence that Antony had been corrupted by his early friends, Curio and Clodius. But in writing his whole life, despite complaints of his 'ostentation', foolish bravery and vain ambition, of his cruel revenge on Cicero for his attacks on him in his Philippic orations, and of his frequent bouts of drunkenness, Plutarch again and again pays grudging tribute to his bravery, his generosity, his patience in adversity, his noble mind, his care of wounded soldiers, and the affection of his men. Some of the characteristics regarded by Plutarch as defects may well have endeared him to Shakespeare. He would, for example, 'jest with one or other . . . drink like a good fellow with everybody . . . sit with the soldiers when they dine, to eat and drink with them soldierlike, it is incredible what wonderful love it won him amongst them'. Shakespeare would hardly have objected to Antony's passing 'away the time in hearing of foolish plays' – both Elizabeth and James offended in the same way – or in his associating with 'players, tumblers, jesters and such sort of people', or to his frequenting of plays while he lived in Greece.

Caesar in the play expressed horror at Antony's lack of dignity in wandering the streets of Alexandria in disguise; but it seems likely that Shakespeare would have been amused by Plutarch's account:

And sometime also, when he would go up and down the city, disguised like a slave in the night, and would peer into poor men's windows and their shops, and scold and brawl with them within the house: and Cleopatra would be also in a chambermaid's array, and amble up and down the streets with him, so that oftentimes Antonius bare away both mocks and blows. Now, though most men misliked this manner, yet the Alexandrians were commonly glad of this jollity, and liked it well, saying very gallantly and wisely: That Antonius shewed them a comical face, to wit, a merry countenance: and the Romans a tragical face, to say, a grim look. (pp. 205–6)[2]

The harmless practical joke played by Cleopatra on Antony when they were angling together is dismissed by Plutarch as a fond (i.e. foolish) and childish pastime. Shakespeare uses it as a treasured memory when Antony is absent from Egypt.

Shakespeare is necessarily selective. He passes over the long account of the Parthian campaign, preferring to link Antony's decline more directly to the relationship with Cleopatra. He also ignored the digression about Timon of Athens. He had already written a play on the subject; the portrait of Antony given by Plutarch did not fit in with that of the great misanthropist; and his decline and fall was not due to man's ingratitude.

Many details of Shakespeare's portrait of Cleopatra were also derived from Plutarch, from the account of her first meeting with Antony to the final scene in the monument. Plutarch points out that her beauty was not unparalleled, but

So sweet was her company and conversation, that a man could not possibly but be taken. And besides her beauty, the good grace she had to talk and discourse, her courteous nature that tempered her words and deeds, was a spur that pricked to the quick. Furthermore, besides all these, her voice and words were marvellous pleasant: for her tongue was an instrument of music to divers sports and pastimes, the which she easily turned to any language that pleased her. (p. 203)

Plutarch goes on to list the many languages for which she did not need an interpreter.

She taunted Antony on occasion, as she does in the first scene of the play, and she frequently teased him. She used many kinds of flattery, devising 'sundry new delights to have Antonius at commandment'. She 'would play at dice with him, drink with him, and hunt commonly with him, and also be with him when he went to any exercise or activity of body'. Plutarch speaks of the various devices she used to prevent Antony from leaving her, and returning to Octavia:

... she subtilly seemed to languish for the love of Antonius, pining her body for lack of meat. Furthermore she every way so framed her countenance, that when Antonius came to see her, she cast her eyes upon him, like a woman ravished for joy. Straight again, when he went from her, she fell a-weeping and blubbering, looked ruefully of the matter, and still found the means that Antonius should oftentimes find her weeping; and then, when he came suddenly upon her, she made as though she dried her eyes, and turned her face away, as if she were unwilling that he should see her weep. (p. 240)

Shakespeare took some hints from this account and used them in the third scene of the play; but although he makes plain, by Cleopatra's own confession to Charmian, that there was an element of play-acting in her behaviour, he does not depict it as mere pretence. When Antony declares that she 'is cunning past man's thought', the cynical Enobarbus demurs: 'alack, sir, no, her passions are made of nothing but the finest part of pure love'. All Plutarch's phrasing, accusing her of insincerity – *seemed, framed, as though, like, as if* – makes us wonder how he knew all this.

Shakespeare had already used the earlier pages of Plutarch's *Life of Marcus Antonius* – up to the defeat of Brutus and Cassius – in *Julius Caesar*, dovetailing them ingeniously with passages from the lives of Brutus and Caesar. One passage from the earlier part, describing the retreat from Modena, is used, as we shall see, as a kind of flashback to Antony's heroic past. All the other incidents of the play are to be found

11

in the later pages of Plutarch's *Life*, although supplemented from other sources.

Although it has often been asserted that Shakespeare was hampered by the inconvenient facts of history, that the play is less well constructed than the other great tragedies, and that it should be classed as that hybrid, a chronicle history, this does less than justice, as we shall see in the next chapter, to Shakespeare's art. Here all that need be said is that he selected his material with care, and that he often modified, purely for dramatic reasons, the raw material he used. One example has already been given: he totally ignored the Parthian campaign.

The play was concerned with the relationship between Antony and Cleopatra and its effect on the struggle between Antony and Caesar for the rule of the whole world. Pompey's threat to the triumvirate was relevant to this struggle because it brought Antony back to Rome. But Shakespeare did not only omit incidents in the interest of the unity of action, he also telescoped those events he dramatized. The prime example is Antony's marriage to Octavia. Reading the play, we may get the impression that Antony returned to Cleopatra soon after the marriage to Octavia. In fact, the marriage lasted several years, and Octavia bore Antony three children. Shakespeare omits these offspring and lets us suppose that the marriage was a failure from the start. This impression is created in the very scene in which the marriage is arranged, for we are immediately reminded of the Cydnus meeting and of Cleopatra's hold on Antony. In the next scene Antony declares that he will return to Egypt, a decision fortified by the Soothsayer; and before the end of the act Enobarbus again asserts that the marriage will be short-lived. We are therefore not surprised when Antony deserts Octavia.

The changes made by Shakespeare do not seriously pervert the facts of history. The death of Fulvia, for example, departs slightly from what actually happened. Plutarch describes how Antony was informed by friends that Fulvia was the cause of the war with Caesar, as she hoped that it would lure him away from Cleopatra: 'But by good fortune, his wife Fulvia going to meet with Antonius, sickened by the way, and died in the city of Sicyone.' Antony had already left Egypt to confer with Caesar, but in the play the news of Fulvia's death reaches Antony in Egypt, and it is used in a dramatic scene with Cleopatra.

A comparison of some passages in the play with North's prose, shows that despite his borrowing of actual words, Shakespeare made significant changes in each case. Antony's last speech (IV.15) owes nearly everything to North's words, and at first sight it looks as if Shakespeare were turning them into verse as economically as possible:

... as for himself, that she should not lament nor sorrow for the miserable change of his fortune at the end of his days; but rather that she should think him the more fortunate for the former triumphs and honours he had received, considering that while he lived he was the noblest and greatest prince of the world, and that now he was overcome not cowardly, but valiantly, a Roman by another Roman. (p. 281)

> The miserable change now at my end
> Lament nor sorrow at; but please your thoughts
> In feeding them with those my former fortunes
> Wherein I lived, the greatest prince o'th'world,
> The noblest; and do now not basely die,
> Not cowardly put off my helmet to
> My countryman; a Roman, by a Roman
> Valiantly vanquished.

Apart from tightening up the sentence-structure, Shakespeare adds two vivid images.

A longer passage is the description of Antony's retreat over the Alps, which Shakespeare puts into Caesar's mouth (I.4) to recall what Antony was like before he had been weakened by his passion for Cleopatra. Caesar and he were then fighting on opposite sides. North's marginal note reads 'Antonius' patience in adversity, notwithstanding his fine bringing up'. The passage runs:

The Senate ... sent Hircius and Pansa, then Consuls, to drive Antonius out of Italy. These two Consuls together with Caesar, who also had an army, went against Antonius that besieged the city of Modena, and there overthrew him in battle. But both the Consuls were slain there. Antonius, flying upon this overthrow, fell into great misery all at once; but the chiefest want of all other, and that pinched him most, was famine. Howbeit he was of such a strong nature that by patience he would overcome any adversity; and the heavier fortune lay upon him, the more constant showed he himself. Every man that feeleth want or adversity knoweth by virtue and discretion what he should do. But when indeed they are overlaid with extremity and be sore oppressed, few have the heart to follow that which they praise and commend, and much less to avoid that they reprove and mislike. But rather, to the contrary, they yield to their accustomed easy life, and through faint heart and lack of courage do change their first mind and purpose. And therefore it was a wonderful example to the soldiers to see Antonius, that was brought up in all fineness and superfluity, so easily to drink puddle water and to eat wild fruits and roots. And moreover it is reported that, even as they passed the Alps, they did eat the barks of trees and such beasts as never man tasted of their flesh before. (p. 192)

Shakespeare naturally omitted the seventy-seven words of moralizing. His other alterations were sometimes condensations. For example, 'brought up in all fineness and superfluity' becomes 'daintily brought up', and 'by patience he would overcome any adversity' becomes 'patience more / Than savages could suffer'. Sometimes he expanded for the sake of vividness or particularity. The reference to famine is turned into a metaphor: 'at thy heel / Did famine follow'; 'puddle water' becomes 'The stale of horses and the gilded puddle / Which beasts would cough at'; 'wild fruits and roots' becomes 'The roughest berry on the rudest hedge'; and 'the barks of trees' becomes

> Yea, like the stag when snow the pasture sheets,
> The banks of trees thou browsèd'st.

The reference to the eating of 'such beasts as never man tasted of their flesh before' becomes the more horrific, 'strange flesh, / Which some did die to look on'.

One of the best-known passages in the play is Enobarbus's account of the first meeting of Antony and Cleopatra (II,2). In its position in the play, after Antony has become betrothed to Octavia, the speech is designed to show that the marriage will inevitably be a failure, and this conviction is made more convincing by Enobarbus's generally critical attitude to Cleopatra.

... she made so light of it and mocked Antonius so much that she disdained to set forward otherwise but to take her barge in the river of Cydnus, the poop whereof was of gold, the sails of purple, and oars of silver, which kept stroke in rowing after the sound of the music of flutes, howboys, citherns, viols, and such other instruments as they played upon in the barge. And now for the person of herself: she was laid under a pavilion of cloth of gold of tissue, apparelled and attired like the goddess Venus commonly drawn in picture; and hard by her, on either hand of her, pretty fair boys apparelled as painters do set forth god Cupid, with little fans in their hands, with the which they fanned wind upon her. Her ladies and gentlewomen also, the fairest of them were apparelled like the nymphs Nereides (which are the mermaids of the waters) and like the Graces, some steering the helm, others tending the tackle and ropes of the barge, out of the which there came a wonderful passing sweet savour of perfumes, that perfumed the wharf's side, pestered with innumerable multitudes of people. Some of them followed the barge all alongst the river's side; others also ran out of the city to see her coming in; so that in the end there ran such multitudes of people one after another to see her that Antonius was left post-alone in the market-place in his imperial seat to give audience. And there went a rumour in the people's mouths that the goddess Venus was come to play with the god Bacchus, for the general good of all Asia. (pp. 201–2)

North's prose can be faulted for structural deficiencies; but the passage gives us an attractive and unforgettable picture of the scene, so that we

have an indelible impression of Cleopatra's enchantment and an understanding of Antony's infatuation. Even the description makes Enobarbus's stage audience almost equally smitten. Shakespeare tightens
up the sentence structure in his version of the incident and omits several
of North's details. He reduces the orchestra to flutes alone (more appropriate, say the critics, to the erotic atmosphere). He omits North's
alternative to the Nereides ('like the Graces') and the rumour concerning
the meeting of Venus and Bacchus. Yet elsewhere he does associate
Venus with Cleopatra, and Bacchus with Antony.

More significant are Shakespeare's numerous additions. Some are
designed to make the description more vivid: the poop of the barge was
made of *beaten* gold; the 'pretty fair boys' become 'pretty *dimpled* boys';
and the 'little fans' become 'divers coloured fans'. Most of the additions,
however, increase the sense of erotic enchantment. The barge 'like a
burnished throne, / Burned on the water'. The sails were 'so perfumèd
that / The winds were love-sick with them'. The water, like a masochistic
woman, was enjoying being beaten by the oars, 'as amorous of their
strokes'. Cleopatra was not merely dressed like Venus, she o'erpictured
'that Venus where we see / The fancy outwork nature'. The wind of the
fans 'did seem / To glow the delicate cheeks which they did cool, / And
what they undid did'. Even the tackle is amorously affected: it is 'silken'
and it swells 'with the touches of those flower-soft hands'. Cleopatra
herself 'beggared all description', a violent metaphor not yet staled by
use and imitation. The perfume 'hits the sense / Of the adjacent wharfs'.
Antony, left alone in the market-place, whistled to the air, which 'but for
vacancy, / Had gone to gaze on Cleopatra too, / And made a gap in
nature'.

All these hyperboles and conceits, put into the mouth of a man whom
the audience takes to be, at least intermittently, a choric character, have
an overwhelming effect. Of course, Enobarbus is enjoying himself. He
has a captive audience in Maecenas and Agrippa, and he makes the most
of his opportunity. But the knowledge that he is exaggerating does not
detract from the effect. It may be mentioned that Enobarbus continues
in the same paradoxical vein when he remarks that Cleopatra made
defect perfection, and that she makes hungry when most she satisfies.

A last example of Shakespeare's use of North's Plutarch is his
adaptation of Charmian's last words (V.2):

One of the soldiers, seeing her, angrily said unto her: 'Is that well done,
Charmion?' 'Very well,' she said again, 'and meet for a princess descended from
the race of so many noble kings.' (p. 292)

FIRST GUARD:
  What work is here, Charmian? Is this well done?
CHARMIAN:
  It is well done, and fitting for a princess
  Descended of so many royal kings.
  Ah, soldier!

T. S. Eliot, perhaps with his tongue in his cheek, remarked that Shakespeare's superiority to the other dramatic versions, all based on Plutarch, was in Charmian's last two words.[3] Shakespeare often drags us back from the world of the theatre to the real world, from dramatis personae to actual people. But there is another significant deviation from North in this passage: he substitutes *royal* for *noble*, because the former had become symbolically significant in the course of the play.[4]

Plutarch's references to the war between Fulvia and Caesar are somewhat obscure; and it was presumably to seek clarification that Shakespeare went to Appian's *Civil Wars* (translated in 1578), a book he had previously consulted during the writing of *Julius Caesar*.[5] There he learnt that Lucius, Antony's brother, had different motives from Fulvia's for the war. Lucius, a staunch republican, was grieved by the fact that the power of the triumvirate had continued 'longer then the time appointed'; but Fulvia, on the other hand, was persuaded 'that if Italy were in quiet, Antony would remain with Cleopatra in Egypt, but if wars were stirred he would come quickly'. When Lucius surrendered to Caesar, he had explained that he had fought so that 'I might have brought the Commonwealth to the rule of the Senate, which is now taken away by the power of three, as thou thyself canst not deny'. This is the point of Antony's words to Caesar: 'Did he not rather / Discredit my authority with yours' (II.2.52–3) and his claim that he was Caesar's partner in the cause against which Lucius fought, 'Your partner in the cause 'gainst which he fought' (II.2.63).

From Appian too Shakespeare picked up some facts about Sextus Pompeius. His growing popularity, recorded by Antony:

> ... The condemned Pompey,
> Rich in his father's honour, creeps apace
> Into the hearts of such, as have not thrived
> Upon the present state ... (I.3.52)

and as reported by the messenger to Caesar:

> ... Pompey is strong at sea,
> And it appears he is beloved of those

> That only have feared Caesar...
> ... flush youth revolt (I.4.36–8, 52)

seems to be based on Appian's account:

Pompey by resort of condemned citizens and ancient possessioners, was greatly increased, both in might and estimation: for they that feared their life, or were spoiled of their goods, or liked not the present state, fled all to him ... beside a repair of young men, desirous of gain and service, not caring under whom they went, because they were all Romans, sought unto him.[6]

Shakespeare casually mentions Pompey's murder (III.5) but leaves the facts obscure. In Goulart's *Life of Octavius* (included in later editions of Plutarch's *Lives*) it is stated that Antony ordered the murder. Appian, however, gives alternative theories of the killing of Pompey by Titius. 'There be that say that Plancus and not Antony did command him to die'; 'some think it was done with Antony's knowledge ... or for Cleopatra'; 'some think that Plancus did it of himself ... that Pompey should give no cause of dissension between Caesar and Antony, or for that Cleopatra would turn her favour to Pompey'. Faced with these rival theories, Shakespeare apparently follows Appian in giving Antony the benefit of the doubt; but as he does not explain what Pompey was doing in the East, the audience is bound to be puzzled by Antony's anger with the officer who murdered him.

There were five plays on the theme of Antony's love for Cleopatra before Shakespeare's. One of them, by Fulke Greville, was destroyed by the author, because he was afraid it might be taken to refer to the Earl of Essex – it is difficult to see why. A second play, by Samuel Brandon, entitled *The Virtuous Octavia*, is so lifeless that no one has suggested that Shakespeare had read it. The other three plays are a different matter: *Antonie* by Robert Garnier, translated by Mary, Countess of Pembroke, as *Antonius* (1592); a sequel, dedicated to the Countess by Samuel Daniel, entitled *Cleopatra* (1594); and the untranslated *Cléopâtre Captive* by Jodelle (1553), which may be a minor source of Shakespeare's play.

The strongest argument that Shakespeare knew *Antonius* is an apparent echo of the Argument to the play, in which it is stated that Antony had married Caesar's sister 'for knitting a straiter bond of amity between them'. So Agrippa, proposing the alliance, says that it would

> ... hold you in perpetual amity
> To make your brothers, and to knit your heart
> With an unslipping knot.

There are several other probable or possible echoes. The first epithet applied to Cleopatra in the first scene of the play is 'tawny', and later Cleopatra confesses that she is 'with Phoebus' amorous pinches black'. Both may have been suggested by the line in *Antonius*:

> And tawny nations scorched with the Sunne (462).

Antony, addressing himself, speaks of how he left Cleopatra:

> Thou breakest at length from thence, as one encharm'd
> Breakes from th'enchaunter that him strongly helde (79–80)

So Shakespeare's Antony resolves in the second scene:

> I must from this enchanting queen break off.

In several places in *Antonius* eyes are compared to suns:

> Her beamy eies, two Sunnes of this our world (715)

> . . . your eies, my Sunne (1595)

> Thy eies, two Sunnes, the lodging place of love
> Which yet for tents to warlike *Mars* did serve. (1941–2)

The Mars–Venus opposition is echoed in the first speech of the play, when Philo complains that Antony's eyes

> That o'er the files and musters of the war
> Have glowed like plated Mars, now bend, now turn
> The office and devotion of their view
> Upon a tawny front.

Cleopatra, in her dream of Antony after his death, thinks of his eyes as

> A sun and moon, which kept their course and lighted
> The little O o'th'earth.

Shakespeare speaks of Nilus' slime, and mentions that the higher the floods, the better the harvest (I.3.69, II.7.21) and both these points are made in the chorus in *Antonius*:

> Where the *Nile*, our father good . . .
> visiting each year the plain . . .
> and with fat slime cov'ring it . . .
> making thereby greatest growe
> busy reapers joyfull paine,
> When his flouds do highest flow. (754–64)

There are several passages in the last act of the play, in which Cleopatra looks forward to rejoining the ghost of Antony: 'By fields whereon the lonely Ghosts do treade' (1833). She urges herself to 'no longer stay / From Antony, who thee at Styx attends' (1908). She asks Antony to 'take me with thee to the hellish plaine, / Thy wife, thy frend' (1950–51) and 'now streight will I die, / And streight with thee a wandring shade will be / Under the *Cypres* tree thou haunt'st alone' (1971–3). With these passages may be compared Cleopatra's 'Husband, I come' and Antony's

> Where souls do couch on flowers, we'll hand in hand,
> And with our sprightly port make the ghosts gaze:
> Dido and her Aeneas shall want troops,
> And all the haunt be ours . . . (IV.14.51–4)[7]

The Countess of Pembroke was an amateur poet, like her brother. Her protegé, Daniel, was a professional, the author of sonnets, moral epistles, long narrative poems, a prose history of England, besides a number of plays. In them he followed the precepts of Sidney and the example of the Countess, making no attempt to write for the public theatre, but adhering to the neo-Senecan style, with narrated action and a chorus after each act. The death of Cleopatra, off-stage, is reported in a speech some 250 lines long. This is the version Shakespeare knew; but in 1607 Daniel revised the play with Cleopatra dying on stage, either because he had heard that Shakespeare's company were putting on a Cleopatra play, or because he had seen it performed. Critics are still divided on which of the two poets was indebted to the other in this particular instance.

Both versions of Daniel's play are concerned with events which took place after the death of Antony. It is, confessedly, a sequel to the Countess's version of Garnier. The portrait of Cleopatra, coming from a notoriously moral poet such as Daniel, is surprisingly favourable. She is deeply concerned about the fate of her children; and, although she laments her former licentiousness

> My vagabond desires no limites found,
> For lust is endlesse, pleasure hath not bound (162–3)

and admits that she did not love Antony until after his death, she now determines to prove by her suicide that she is worthy of him.

There are many points in the early version of Daniel's play which Shakespeare appears to have remembered. Cleopatra's reluctance to have Octavia a witness of her misery, 'That I should passe whereas *Octavia* stands / To view my miserie that purchas'd hers' (70); her declaration that she has 'both hands and will' to kill herself (54); her reference to her 'new appeering wrinckles of declining' (171); her statement to Proculeius that 'she craved not life, but leave to die' (288); her reference to herself as spouse (1104) and wife (1133) – these are some of the phrases and words which may have caught Shakespeare's eye. More significant is Cleopatra's excuse for concealing the full amount of her treasure:

> If I reserv'd some certaine womens toyes . . .
> But what I kept, I kept to make my way
> Unto thy *Livia* and *Octavias* grace,
> That thereby in compassion mooved, they
> Might mediate thy favour in my case. (679ff)

So Shakespeare's Cleopatra confesses that she has kept back

> Immoment toys . . .
> Some nobler token I have kept apart
> For Livia and Octavia, to induce
> Their mediation. (V.2.166ff)

In the messenger's long account of Cleopatra's suicide, he compares her rich array to the garments she wore on the Cydnus: 'Even as she went at first to meete her love' (1464). So Shakespeare's heroine declares:

> I am again for Cydnus
> To meet Mark Antony. (V.2.228–9)

Although Plutarch mentions that Dolabella 'did bear no evil will unto Cleopatra', Daniel makes him fall in love with her, so that he is reproved by Caesar:

> What, in a passion, *Dolabella*? what, take heed:
> Let others' fresh examples be thy warning;
> What mischiefes these so idle humors breed,
> Whilst error keepes us from a true discerning. (722–5)

Dolabella nevertheless writes to her; and Cleopatra, reading his letter, asks: 'What hath my face yet powre to win a Lover' (1069), and she adds: 'I must die his debtor.' Shakespeare echoes these words in 'Dolabella, I shall remain your debtor'. In his treatment of the Dolabella episode, Shakespeare is much closer to Daniel than he is to Plutarch.

A last example of Daniel's influence is in the scene which follows Cleopatra's death. Plutarch mentions that Charmion was trimming the Queen's diadem. Daniel describes how Cleopatra in

> her sinking downe she wries
> The Diadem which on her head shee wore,
> Which *Charmion* (poor weake feeble maid) espies,
> And hastes to right it as it was before. (1635-8)

So Shakespeare's Charmian says:

> Your crown's awry;
> I'll mend it, and then play –

Cleopatra is essentially a closet drama, designed for reading. The speeches are inordinately long. Except for one short scene between Cleopatra and Caesar there is no real confrontation. The action takes place off-stage and is apparently regarded by Daniel as a regrettable necessity, and much less interesting than the moralizing it evokes. The chorus takes no part in the action and its comments are elegantly trite. Even the man who brings the asps turns out to be a servant in disguise. The heroine is dignified and loses her cool only when she is exposed by her treasurer. She exhibits none of the infinite variety of Shakespeare's character, and little of her fascination; but as Daniel was concerned only with the last few hours of her life, this is less of a handicap than it would otherwise have been. The language of the play earned Coleridge's praise; but it is nevertheless remarkable that Shakespeare was able to take so many hints from so unpromising a source and develop them into some of the greatest dramatic poetry in English or, one imagines, in any language.[8]

Another of Daniel's works, *A Letter from Octavia to Marcus Antonius* (1599), also left its mark on Shakespeare's play. In the prose Argument it is said that Antony, 'having yet upon him the fetters of Egypt, could admit no new laws into the state of his affection' and Shakespeare's Antony decides in the second scene of the play:

> These strong Egyptian fetters I must break,
> Or lose myself in dotage.

We have suggested that Shakespeare had read the essay in Plutarch's *Morals* on Isis and Osiris and that a book he knew well, *The Golden Ass* of Apuleius, provided him with more background information about the worship of Isis.[9]

More significant, perhaps, is the resemblance between the stories of Dido and Cleopatra. The Romans themselves were aware of these resemblances. In both stories a famous soldier, credited with divine ancestry (Aeneas from Venus, Antony from Hercules) falls in love with an

African queen, who is a widow. On receiving a divine command to proceed to Italy, Aeneas unwillingly deserts Dido, who forthwith commits suicide; but Antony, initially obeying the call of duty, afterwards returns to Cleopatra. Aeneas becomes the founder of Rome, Antony ultimately becomes its enemy.

Elizabethan schoolboys would be acquainted with both stories, and schoolmasters could hardly refrain from pointing out the moral: that public duty should come before private pleasure, and even before personal fidelity. Shakespeare mentions Dido in several of his plays, from *Romeo and Juliet* to *The Tempest*; he imitates Aeneas's account of the fall of Troy in the second act of *Hamlet* and of Marlowe's version of it in *Dido, Queen of Carthage*. It has been argued by Brian Gibbons [10] that 'the quality and dramatic effect of Dido's sublime erotic rhetoric informs the inner life and movement of Cleopatra's poetic imagination'. He mentions, too, Cleopatra's 'alternating warmth and coldness to Antony'; her unpredictable capriciousness and her treatment of the messenger who brings news of Antony's marriage, which is comparable with Dido's treatment of the Nurse who brings her bad tidings. Some of Marlowe's lines seem to be echoed in Shakespeare's, notably when Dido exclaims, 'In his looks I see eternity' and Cleopatra tells Antony, 'Eternity was in our lips and eyes'. It is not surprising, therefore, that Antony before his suicide should imagine an encounter with Dido and Aeneas in the underworld, and suppose that Cleopatra and he would outshine them, 'and all the haunt be ours'.

2. Construction

We have seen in the previous chapter what materials were available to Shakespeare in constructing the play, and we are now in a position to consider what use he made of them. But first it will be necessary to discuss at what point in Shakespeare's career the play was written.

The exact date of the first performance of *Antony and Cleopatra* is not known. It must have been before 20 May 1608, because on that date it was entered in the Stationers' Register. This was a necessary preliminary to publication; but it was often done to prevent unauthorized publication, and fifteen years elapsed before *Antony and Cleopatra* appeared in the First Folio, the collection of thirty-six plays, which was published in 1623, seven years after Shakespeare's death. The absence of any edition in his lifetime does not indicate that the play was comparatively unpopular, since there were no separate editions of *As You Like It*, *Twelfth Night*, *Coriolanus* and *The Tempest* – to name no others – before 1623. Nor should too much be deduced from the fact that Burbage is not mentioned in connection with the part of Antony, as he is with Othello.

All the evidence suggests that the play was written soon after *King Lear* and *Macbeth* (1604–6) when Shakespeare was at the height of his powers, and not long before the last of the Roman plays, *Coriolanus*. As one source of *Timon of Athens* was Plutarch's *Life of Marcus Antonius* (see p. 10), *Antony and Cleopatra* may have been written either just before, or more probably just after that play. As we have seen, it is not known whether Daniel's revision of his *Cleopatra* preceded or followed Shakespeare's play; but it is safe to assume that its first performance was not long before May 1608.

The play was printed from Shakespeare's manuscript – not from the prompt copy – and there are a number of obscurities, due either to Shakespeare's oversights or to the illegibility of his handwriting. Many of these would have been ironed out in the course of production. Examples are the mute characters in the second scene of the play, the entrance of 'three or four' servants in IV.2, when more are manifestly required, the awkward repetition of 'I am dying, Egypt, dying', and the precise way in which Cleopatra was surprised and captured. The text also contains a considerable number of misprints which have exercised the ingenuity of editors; and we have to remember that readings which have not been suspected, because they make satisfactory sense, may not

23

have been what Shakespeare wrote. (Emrys Jones accepts one emendation which was not made until 1961.) But the most important fact about the text of the play is that it was not divided into acts, and that even the scenes are not marked. The division into five acts and forty-two scenes by subsequent editors has done much to foster the view that the play lacks unity, that it has the ramshackle construction of a chronicle play, and that it completely lacks the tightly knit structure of *Othello* or *Macbeth*. (Nevertheless, we have, for ease of reference, retained the traditional act divisions. Yet we should continually remember that Shakespeare was guiltless of them.)

When Dryden wrote *All for Love* in avowed imitation of *Antony and Cleopatra*, he tried to remedy what he regarded as its defects by reconstructing the plot so that it obeyed as far as possible the neoclassical unities of Time, Place and Action. The whole action is set in Alexandria, so that the unity of place is satisfied. Dryden does not, like Shakespeare, jump from Egypt to Rome and from Italy to Greece. Nor does he deal with events that occupied a dozen years; but, concentrating on the last hours of the protagonists, he tries to keep within the time required by the purists; and he sought to preserve the unity of action by virtually ignoring the power struggle and concentrating on love. Caesar does not appear; but Octavia arrives with her children on a secret visit to Alexandria, in an attempt to win back Antony. These expedients make *All for Love* a travesty of history beside which *Antony and Cleopatra* is a model of discretion.

There was another reason why Dryden thought he could improve on Shakespeare and why he regarded the multiple scenes of *Antony and Cleopatra* as dramatically unsatisfactory. Although only sixty years separated the two plays, there had been a theatrical revolution – as well as a political one – in the interim. The stage for which Shakespeare's plays were written, whether the Globe or Blackfriars, was essentially a platform thrust out into the audience, and at the Globe most of them stood. There was no curtain and no painted scenery, and therefore no need for intervals during which the sets could be changed. The nature of the stage was radically transformed by the introduction of a proscenium arch, a curtain, artificial lighting and scenery. On such a stage the twenty-eight scenes of Acts III and IV presented a real problem; and when editors attached locations to the various scenes – Syria, Rome, Alexandria, Athens, Actium – the problem became insoluble, especially if audiences expected to see pictures of the Parthenon or the pyramids. If the play were to be performed in the new playhouses, it would have to be cut to ribbons and radically altered, so as to avoid intolerable waits between scenes. Shakespeare's audience did not need representations of the Acropolis or the Capitol to know the location. Where necessary, Shakespeare informs us of the location by ostensibly casual references in the dialogue. Three examples will suffice: 'Now, darting Parthia' (III.1.1); 'Bear me, good friends, where Cleopatra bides' (IV.14.131); 'Look out o'th'other side your monument' (IV.15.7).

The difference between the Elizabethan stage and that of the eighteenth and nineteenth centuries account, no doubt, for the failure of two great critics to appreciate Shakespeare's methods in *Antony and Cleopatra*. Samuel Johnson, who was liberal enough in his views to excuse Shakespeare for not obeying the unities, complained that the events 'are produced without any art of connection or care of disposition'; and A. C. Bradley, an ardent playgoer, complained of its defective construction. He thought that there was little action in the first three acts, and that the first half of the play was not tragic in tone. It is a strange estimate of the first three acts, which include Antony's leaving Egypt, marrying Octavia, patching up peace with Pompey, quarrelling with Caesar, returning to Egypt, and being defeated at Actium. On one point Bradley is surely mistaken. He complains that we do not see the inner struggles of the characters; but we see the process of Cleopatra's transformation, of Enobarbus's desertion and subsequent remorse, and of Antony's vacillation between the pursuit of power and the enchantment of Cleopatra. We do not see the actual arrival of Antony in Egypt – why should we? What matters is the moment when he decides to return. This decision was not made after the fifth scene in Act III, as Bradley apparently assumes, but long before in the Soothsayer scene. But the idea that the construction of the play was defective dies hard, despite Harley Granville-Barker's defence in his Preface. Shakespeare's critics should have recalled the way in which the heroine made defect perfection.

Even as late as 1970 French's Acting Edition of the play, intended for amateur dramatic societies, included fifteen different sets, and twice that number of scene changes; but the editor, George Skillan, a skilled and experienced actor, admitted that the painted scenery could 'be dispensed with either in part or entirely'. He was well aware of the danger of slowing down the action by scene changes, but he seems not to have realized that there was a positive advantage in dispensing with scenery – that Shakespeare provided verbal scene-painting with which actual painting might well conflict, and which would at any rate be superfluous.

Leaving aside for the moment the question of unity, it is clear that the sense we get in watching the play that great public and historical issues are at stake could not have been so vividly brought home to us if

Shakespeare had restricted the setting to Alexandria. The fact that we are transported to the four corners of the Roman world is a forcible reminder of the extent and importance of that world. It was, in fact, the world. Shakespeare wasn't writing an historical play, but his sense of history is vital to his conception. The summary of the actual historical events (see p. 118) shows that Shakespeare was remarkably true to the spirit, if not to the details, of history.

With the deliberate violation of the unity of place went the abolition of the unity of time. Emrys Jones in *Scenic Form in Shakespeare* commented on the frequent mention of the time taken for the numerous journeys:

This way of stressing geographical distances and the time taken to traverse them alerts us to what was after all for the persons of the history, an irreducible and unignorable reality – the physical milieu in which they lived and which they took for granted. It reminds us that these persons were actual human beings, not mere characters in a story.

One cannot travel such distances, even by Concorde, and keep within the neoclassical rules; and, of course, the spread of the action over many years increases our apparent involvement in the movement of history. *Antony and Cleopatra* is, in a sense, epic drama, although very different from the epic drama of the present century.

How, then, does Shakespeare prevent the play from being a chronicle history – a throw-back to his earliest historical dramas, the three parts of *Henry VI*. A few critics have even claimed that *King Lear*, the masterpiece of construction, was really a chronicle play. But in *Antony and Cleopatra* every scene, whatever its setting, continually alludes to the contending principles of love and power. We are never allowed to forget Rome in Egypt, or Egypt in Rome. In the very first scene the central dialogue of the lovers is framed by the disapproving comments of Philo and Demetrius (see p. 68). What is more, the lovers' dialogue is precisely about the relative merits of love and empire, and it is interrupted by news from Rome. Cleopatra jeers at Antony's position in relation to Caesar and so provokes him to reject Rome and its empire.

The second scene, although mainly designed to exhibit the Egyptian way of life, introduces a prophecy that Charmian would outlive Cleopatra, and this is duly fulfilled at the end of the play; and in the latter part of the scene Antony listens to the news from Rome, the success of the Parthians, the threat from Pompey, the death of Fulvia – any one of which would necessitate his return to Rome. In the third scene he breaks the news to Cleopatra. In the fourth scene, in Rome, the sole topic of conversation is Antony's 'lascivious wassails' contrasted with his former renown as a soldier. In the fifth scene Cleopatra talks of her relations with Antony and receives a present from him. The same method is followed throughout the play, the scenes alternating for the most part between Egypt and Italy, until Act IV when the setting is Egypt throughout. In the first scene of Act II, for example, Pompey hopes that Antony will not leave Egypt, although the audience knows that he is already on his way to Rome. In the scene where the marriage with Octavia is arranged, Egypt is kept in our minds by Enobarbus's description of the Cydnus meeting. In the next scene Antony is advised by the Soothsayer to return to Egypt, and Egypt and Cleopatra are the main topics of conversation during the last two scenes of the act.

Meanwhile we have had one of Shakespeare's most daring devices. Cleopatra has her first interview with the Messenger who brings her news of Antony's marriage in II.5. Five scenes later (III.3) she has her second interview with the Messenger, and this follows chronologically only a few minutes after the first. She had instructed Alexas to get the Messenger to give a full report on Octavia and the Messenger is brought in to give the report in person. Between these two scenes Caesar and Antony have signed a peace treaty with Pompey; Pompey has played host to the triumvirs on his galley; Ventidius, despatched to Parthia in II.4, has returned victorious in III.1; Antony has left Rome with his bride. Shakespeare has played fast and loose with time, with all the freedom of a television director. The reason is simple. As Granville-Barker pointed out,[1] Shakespeare had more Roman than Egyptian material in the first part of the play and he had the problem of keeping Cleopatra in the forefront of our minds:

all the story asks is that she should be left by Antony, and then sit waiting, patiently or impatiently, for his return ... Shakespeare lets the impulse of his opening carry him to the point of Antony's departure ... till he has his story's master-motive made fertile in our minds.

When Cleopatra hears of Antony's marriage, there is no more Egyptian material left, so 'this episode is split up and spread over two scenes'. Thereafter, until Antony returns to Egypt, the Roman material is drastically compressed and mostly reported. Antony's return to Cleopatra is reported by Caesar, not to him, and not shown on the stage.

Everything is designed to bring out the conflict between Caesar and Antony, and between Rome and Egypt, and the principles for which they stand. There is, for example, a subtle use of local colour. From the first scene to the last we unconsciously absorb the differences between the two ways of life. In the first scene Antony and Cleopatra appear fanned by eunuchs. In the second scene there are references to the overflowing Nile and three invocations of Isis. In the third scene Antony swears by 'the fire that quickens Nilus' slime'. In the fourth scene Caesar provides us with a scathing account of the way Antony spends his time, implying all the time that it violated Roman codes of conduct. In the next scene Cleopatra converses with a eunuch and refers to Antony's description of her as 'my serpent of old Nile'. So one could go on throughout the play, calling attention to similar touches. Antony describes the flooding of the Nile (II.7) and the way it affects the harvest, and he pulls Lepidus's leg about the crocodile. Caesar complains of Cleopatra impersonating Isis (III.6), blessed, no doubt, by the admiring priests; and Cleopatra, accused of flirting with Thidias, speaks of lying graveless 'till the flies and gnats of Nile / Have buried' all her offspring and all her brave Egyptians (III.13). In the last scene it is the 'pretty worm of Nilus' which enables her to obtain a painless death and so defeat Caesar.

As the play covers a period of several years, it is bound to seem episodic; but the various episodes all contribute to the design of the whole. Several of them could almost be regarded as one-act plays, and, considered in isolation – as they must not be – those in which Cleopatra is the protagonist are often comic in their effect. This has worried those critics who object to a mingling of tragedy and comedy. The first playlet we might isolate concerns Antony's departure from Egypt (I.3). Cleopatra outlines her strategy to Charmian: to be docile is the way to lose him. So, realizing that Antony intends to leave Egypt, Cleopatra takes the offensive, attacking her lover for his 'betrayal', quoting at him his former vows; and when she hears of Fulvia's death, which Antony thinks will prove that he is not deserting Cleopatra, she rounds on him for his heartlessness in not grieving for his wife. But she realizes that she has overstepped the mark when she mocks his descent from Hercules, and she apologizes:

> But, sir, forgive me,
> Since my becomings kill me, when they do not
> Eye well to you.

So, at the end of the scene, Cleopatra bows to the inevitable, but with Antony not really breaking his Egyptian fetters.

The second playlet concerns Cleopatra and the Messenger. She vents her wrath on the bearer of ill tidings, striking him twice, seizing him by the hair, and drawing a knife to kill him (II.5). After being guilty of inflicting grievous bodily harm, she is ashamed of her conduct. In the second interview she questions the Messenger on her rival (III.3). The belated diplomacy of the Messenger, assisted by the assurances and flattery of Charmian and Iras, lead to a complete reversal of Cleopatra's attitude. The tone of the episode is broadly comic.

A third playlet is the attempt by Thidias to persuade Cleopatra to betray Antony. It is preceded by a prologue (III.12) in which Caesar offers peace to Egypt, on condition, as Antony puts it, that his grizzled head is sent to Caesar. He, or Shakespeare, is thinking of the treacherous way in which Pompey's grizzled head was sent to Julius Caesar – one of the best-known episodes in Roman history. After this prologue we may be wondering if Cleopatra will buy peace at this price. The next scene begins as comedy, but changes to tragi-comedy because of Antony's violent jealousy. When Cleopatra welcomes Thidias, Enobarbus assumes that she is deserting Antony – despite her willingness to have the interview in the presence of Antony's friends. The audience has come to regard Enobarbus as a reliable commentator; so we may, at first, share his suspicions. But Cleopatra's 'O!' and 'mine honour was not yielded, / But conquered merely' can hardly be spoken without her conveying to the audience, though not to Thidias, her ironical amusement. It is noteworthy that in her reply to Thidias, when he asks her to leave Antony and put herself under Caesar's shroud, she evades answering the real question. She knows that Egypt is at Caesar's mercy and she tries to get what she can from submission. Possibly she thinks that wheedling Thidias is a means of deceiving Caesar. In any case she cannot resist the temptation of trying to attract any personable young man.

When Antony arrives on the scene he is, for the first time in the play, extremely jealous. He does not really think that Cleopatra is likely to betray him to Caesar, but he is outraged that she could give favours to Thidias in order to flatter Caesar. The sight of Thidias kissing her hand sparks off an explosion of his repressed doubts about the woman for whom he has sacrificed so much. He remembers her succession of lovers before he met her – Julius Caesar, Pompey and others 'unregistered in vulgar fame'; he feels once more that the bond between them is merely lust, 'th'expense of spirit in a waste of shame'; he feels a pang of guilt at his treatment of Octavia and at the loss of ordinary domestic life. Above all, perhaps, he feels that he has been metaphorically cuckolded by a much younger man. Hence the whipping of Thidias, the psychological necessity of proving him effeminate, and hence the callous suggestion that Caesar should take revenge on Hipparchus. During his long outburst and savage invective, Cleopatra makes five attempts to speak, but finally confesses that she must 'stay his time'. At last, when Antony for the first time poses a direct question, she asks in reply, 'Not know me yet?' And when he asks, 'Cold-hearted toward me?', she is able to convince him of the absurdity of the question. They are reconciled. They decide to have one other – the last? – gaudy night. But to Enobarbus, Antony's restored confidence is a proof that his valour is preying on his reason. Loyal up till now, Enobarbus decides to desert, at the very time the audience's faith in Cleopatra's loyalty is restored.

The fourth of the Cleopatra playlets consists of her single meeting with Caesar (V.2). We are again confronted with doubts about her motivation. Is she prepared to come to terms with Caesar? Would she agree to go on living if she could be assured that she would not have to grace Caesar's triumph as its star attraction? Does she finally kill herself, not for love of Antony, but because she cannot dissuade Caesar? Is the scene with Seleucus a charade to delude Caesar, arranged beforehand, or is Seleucus himself completely innocent, so that his surprise is genuine and convincing to Caesar? These are questions which every director, and every actress, must answer.

Plutarch makes it clear that Caesar thought he was deceiving Cleopatra about his intentions, 'being himself deceived'. This is probably how Shakespeare meant the scene to be played. It is made clear by Cleopatra's first words after Caesar's exit. 'He words me . . . that I should not / Be noble to myself.' Immediately she instructs Charmian about making arrangements for the suicide, and Iras says 'Finish, good lady'. But the scene is best played with Seleucus not let into the secret, and thinking that he is betraying his mistress.

The scene opens with Caesar having to ask, or pretending that he cannot distinguish Cleopatra from her attendants: 'Which is the Queen of Egypt?' Cleopatra kneels and acts the part of a humble and penitent woman, confessing to those sexual frailties which 'Have often shamed our sex', and which, she knows, have shocked Caesar. Caesar, also acting a role, promises to extenuate her faults, but then makes the blunder of threatening to murder her children if she commits suicide.

Cleopatra's underestimate of her treasure and her calculated rage with Seleucus are designed to convince Caesar that she intends to live. Why should she bother about keeping some of her treasure if she intended to die? Caesar is lulled into a false sense of security, and Cleopatra's suspicions about Caesar's intentions are promptly confirmed by Dolabella.

Cleopatra's encounter with Dolabella is another episode worth discussing. As we have seen (p. 20), although Dolabella was a favourite of Caesar's, he was also, according to Plutarch, well disposed to Cleopatra.

Daniel expanded this hint and made him positively enamoured, and
Shakespeare accepted this interpretation. Antony had advised Cleopatra
to trust only Proculeius, who is responsible for her capture. Some critics
contrast his loyalty to Caesar with Dolabella's treachery in revealing his
master's intentions. J. Leeds Barroll says that by 'putting Cleopatra
before his political duty, he violates the high trust implicit in Caesar's
commands to him at the very end of the play'.[2] There are occasions,
however, as civil servants have found in our day, when a violation of
trust can be regarded as positively laudable. Dolabella, moreover, knows
that he can receive no reward from the Queen for his services.

The scene begins with Proculeius instructing Dolabella to be gentle
with Cleopatra, and she asks Proculeius to inform Caesar of her wish to
die, in the heat of the moment unwisely disclosing her intention to
Caesar. Dolabella addresses her as 'Most noble Empress' (her rank),
'most sovereign creature' (her appearance and personality) and finally
by her name, while she is recounting her ecstatic dream of Antony.
When she asks Dolabella,

> Think you there was or might be such a man
> As this I dreamt of?

he replies, as gently as possible, 'Gentle madam, no'; but he falls in love
with her because he recognizes the depth of her love for Antony:

> Would I might never
> O'ertake pursued success but I do feel,
> By the rebound of yours, a grief that smites
> My very heart at root.

Immediately Cleopatra obtains the information she needs: that Caesar is
going to have her in his triumph. Dolabella returns after the Seleucus
episode to confirm what he had revealed:

> Madam, as thereto sworn, by your command,
> Which my love makes religion to obey.

She had not commanded him, nor had he sworn: both command and
oath were imaginary fruits of his love and compassion. He knows that
the only reward he will obtain from her is gratitude – 'I shall remain
your debtor', as she says. Although Daniel's Caesar reproves him,
Shakespeare's apparently does not suspect that he has leaked the information to Cleopatra.

In discussing Enobarbus's character, we commented on his gradual
decision to leave Antony, and his remorse afterwards. His desertion

forms a little play in itself. He first exhibits serious disagreement with Antony when he objects to Cleopatra's presence in the war, and even more strongly to the decision to fight at sea. He is horrified by the flight of Cleopatra's ships at Actium, and still more by Antony's following her, although this proves that his advice was sound. Despite the decision of Canidius to desert, Enobarbus, against his reason and self-interest, decides to stay with Antony. This decision is gradually eroded by Antony's foolish deeds – his absurd challenge to Caesar, his request to live a private man in Athens, his alternation of pessimism and bravado. But Enobarbus, knowing it to be foolish from the worldly point of view, declares that

> he that can endure
> To follow with allegiance a fallen lord
> Does conquer him that did his master conquer
> And earns a place i'th'story. (III.13)

But after the Thidias episode, recognizing Antony's disintegration, Enobarbus decides to 'seek some way to leave him'.

All this is a prologue to his actual desertion. We next see him after the event, and he immediately suffers two shocks. The first is his realization that even from the standpoint of self-interest he has blundered. Alexas, who had persuaded Herod to change sides, has been hanged; Canidius, who deserted early, has been given no honourable trust; and the deserters are to be put in the front line of battle, so that they will be fighting their former comrades. Enobarbus admits his mistake. The second shock comes with the arrival of his treasure, augmented by Antony. 'Your emperor', says one of Caesar's soldiers, 'continues still a Jove'. Antony's magnanimity heaps coals of fire on Enobarbus's head. Bitterly ashamed of his own turpitude, he feels that his heart has broken. And so he dies mysteriously, not, as in Plutarch, of an ague, but of shame. He asks Antony's forgiveness (which he already has) but wishes everyone else not to forgive him, but to regard him as the lowest of mankind, a runaway slave, 'A master-leaver and a fugitive'. It is a dramatic reversal. The cynical observer who believed that he, like everyone else, should pursue self-interest, has been converted by Antony's greatness of heart, his magnanimity, into a repentant sinner. The conversion looks forward to the transformation of Cleopatra; and this is a good example of the way in which individual episodes must be considered in relation to the design of the whole play.

The short dialogue between two minor characters, Pompey and Menas, is another example. It is complete in itself; it passes like a flash in the revels on Pompey's galley; but yet it throws a blinding light on the world of power in which Caesar is wholly, and Antony and Cleopatra partially, involved. Pompey, until this scene on board his galley, has claimed to be one of the justest men (II.1.2) and a champion of the republican cause for which his father, as well as Brutus and Cato, had died. But he has accepted the bribe of Sicily and Sardinia; and now Menas offers to make him 'lord of the whole world', by cutting the throats of his guests. His answer is revealing: he would have approved of the murder if he had not been given warning.

> Ah, this thou shouldst have done,
> And not have spoke on't! In me 'tis villainy;
> In thee't had been good service . . .
>   . . . Being done unknown,
> I should have found it afterwards well done,
> But must condemn it now.

He claims that his honour is more important to him than his interest, not the other way round; but he is quite willing to profit from a murder committed for him by someone else. For once one agrees with Elizabeth Griffith who declared in 1775 about this episode that

. . . in morals, there is no difference between the receiver and the thief; and as the wages of sin are pronounced to be death, in the Scripture sense of the word, the delinquent who accepts the emoluments of vice must expect to be included under the same sentence.[3]

In this dialogue Menas, although a scoundrel, appears as the more honest, as well as the more ruthless man. The scene, it should be added, owes much of its power to the convivial setting: Menas is the one sober person on the boat.

A last example may be given of Shakespeare's scenic art – Antony's suicide. It begins with his fury at the surrender of the fleet, for which he thinks Cleopatra was responsible. He terrifies her by his rage and resolves that 'the witch shall die'. He calls for Eros, and in the moments before he answers the call, Cleopatra sends Mardian to announce her death. The sequence of events is very closely knit, for before Mardian's arrival with the announcement, Antony tells Eros that he has lost his identity because of his disillusionment with Cleopatra: he resolves to kill her and then commit suicide. The report of her death makes him exonerate her, and he has no hesitation about what he must do:

> Unarm, Eros. The long day's task is done,
> And we must sleep.

The request to Eros to kill him, in accordance with his oath, apparently reminded Shakespeare of two parallel scenes in *Julius Caesar*, in which Cassius and Brutus both ask soldiers to slay them, and so prevent them from falling alive into their enemies' hands. Pindarus reluctantly kills Cassius, but Brutus's request is refused by three soldiers in turn before Strato finally agrees.

Antony's attempt at suicide is bungled, not because Shakespeare wanted to underline Antony's incompetence, but because, closely following Plutarch, he had to have a final meeting between the lovers. Before that takes place Antony is informed that Cleopatra is alive. He does not utter then or later a single word of reproach for her deception. Although his immediate motive for suicide had proved false, there was still an overwhelming motive which he shared with Brutus, Cassius, Cato and other famous Romans.

It is in this scene that Antony's demi-godlike status is stressed. He compares his situation to that of Hercules, dying in the poisoned shirt of Nessus; and his soldiers inadvertently forestall the Revelation's mysterious words that 'The star is fallen' and 'Time is at his period'.[4]

Although, for purposes of analysis, one can divide the play into a large number of separate scenes, they are not, of course, complete in themselves. Each one gains significance from its position in the total design of the play, and in the continual development of the relationship between the protagonists. As Emrys Jones remarks, the scenes 'for all their concern with rendering the random flow of events, they are in fact exquisitely ordered; the sequence is a marvel of minute plotting'.[5] He goes on to warn that the impression we get of the 'illusion of life-likeness' should not lead us to ignore 'the reality of formidable artistry'.

It is certainly true that Shakespeare's use of dozens of short scenes is essential to his purposes. Only thus could he convey what is his grandest attempt to present a drama of personal relationship in a panorama of world affairs. He had dealt with the inextricability of the public and the personal in the increasingly subtle series of the English Histories; but the Wars of the Roses, the battle of Agincourt, and the advent of the Tudors, though important to Englishmen, are in the context of world history almost provincial. Shakespeare had dealt brilliantly with political problems in *Julius Caesar*, but the personal lives of Brutus and Caesar are of minor importance, and we hear nothing at all of the private lives of Antony and Cassius. The impossibility of divorcing private from public is apparent in *Macbeth*, and in *King Lear* the fate of the country depends on a family quarrel. But in *Antony and Cleopatra* for the first time

Shakespeare dramatized one of the turning points of world history and showed how its outcome depended on the ambitions, the emotions, the animosities, the loves, the mistakes of individuals, and partly on accident. Without the variety of setting and the long period of time covered by the play, Shakespeare could not have succeeded in his aim. For anything of comparable range one would have to go to Shakespeare's arch-enemy, Tolstoy, whose *War and Peace* has a scope as vast. That Shakespeare could compress his huge theme into the three hours' traffic of the stage was an additional miracle of art.

As we have seen, the art was not fully appreciated by Johnson and Bradley, because they did not realize that Shakespeare substituted a unity of design for a unity of action. As Ernest Schanzer pointed out, 'nowhere is this principle of construction better illustrated than in *Antony and Cleopatra*'. The structural pattern, he claims, 'is most perfectly adjusted to the theme' and the pattern consists of contrasts between Rome and Egypt, and parallels between the lovers who frequently echo each other's words, and at the end, each other's deeds.[6]

We may add here a remark by John Danby: 'To describe the swiftness of *Antony and Cleopatra* we need to draw on the imagery of the cinema. There is more cinematic movement, more panning, tracking and playing with the camera, more mixing of shots than in any other of Shakespeare's tragedies'.[7] This is one reason why the play is more easily appreciated in 1986 than it was a hundred years ago.

3. Characterization

This chapter should be regarded as a supplement to the Commentary in which attention will be called to significant acts and words of the various characters.

As in all Shakespeare's plays, there is in *Antony and Cleopatra* a great variety of characterization, ranging from the complex and detailed portraits of the protagonists to the faceless walking-on parts, such as Lamprius, Rannius and Lucillius in the second scene of the play, who are given no words to speak and are so shadowy that they are omitted from most editions. Then there is the difference between the choric commentators who are circumscribed by their comments – Demetrius and Philo exist merely to express the Roman view of Antony – and other characters who seem to be created to fit the situation in which they find themselves, such as the Clown who brings the figs to Cleopatra. In other words, Shakespeare started from a story, a series of events in a causal sequence, provided largely by the facts of history, and he created characters uniquely suitable to the roles they had to play. Yet characters who began like this would often take on a life of their own.

Enobarbus

We may begin with Enobarbus, a prominent figure who appears in no less than twelve scenes. Historically he was a professional soldier who had had an important command under Pompey at the battle of Pharsalia. If Shakespeare knew this fact from Plutarch's *Life* of Pompey, he would know that Enobarbus had changed sides and was not unduly concerned with the rights and wrongs of the side for which he was fighting. In the *Life* of Antony Domitius Enobarbus is introduced merely as an illustration of the hero's generosity:

He dealt very friendly and courteously with Domitius, and against Cleopatra's mind. For he being sick of an ague when he took a little boat to go unto Caesar's camp, Antonius was very sorry for it, but yet he sent after him all his carriage, train and men: and the same Domitius, as though he gave him to understand that he repented his open treason, he died immediately after.

Plutarch implies that Enobarbus died of an ague. Shakespeare does not mention this illness and allows us to understand that the cause of death was remorse. The other pointer to Enobarbus's character was the fact that Cleopatra disapproved of Antony's generosity to him. Shakespeare does not mention this; but from it he deduced that Enobarbus was critical of Cleopatra and of Antony's infatuation. It was not much to go on; but from this sketchy outline Shakespeare created one of his most memorable characters (perhaps Ralph Richardson's finest part at the Old Vic.) His first appearance (I.2) is not particularly memorable. He is there to take part in characteristic Alexandrian revels, which turn out to be remarkably decorous; he orders the servants to bring enough wine to drink Cleopatra's health, and his only remark about the fortune-telling, of which he is sceptical, is to foretell: 'Mine, and most of our fortunes, tonight shall be drunk to bed'. In the later part of the scene, in his conversation with Antony, he displays more individuality. When Antony informs him that they are to leave Egypt, he exhibits his humorous cynicism, his delight in bawdy innuendos, his scorn of humbug, as when he says of Fulvia's death, 'the tears live in an onion that should water this sorrow', and his feeling that women, however pleasurable, are less important than public affairs: 'between them and a great cause they should be esteemed nothing'. He is therefore relieved by Antony's decision to leave Egypt – a decision he can make only by denigrating Cleopatra. It is left to Enobarbus, despite his low opinion of women, to defend her from Antony's accusation that 'she is cunning past man's thought'. 'Alack, sir, no,' Enobarbus replies, 'her passions are made of nothing but the finest part of pure love.' But then he proceeds to indulge in such exaggerations about her storms and tempests that we wonder whether he really believes that her behaviour is not calculated. In proving her lack of cunning, he inadvertently proves the opposite.

We next meet Enobarbus in Rome (II.2) when he refuses Lepidus's request that he should advise Antony to use 'soft and gentle speech'. At this point in the play he is an enthusiastic partisan. He is too much of a realist not to know that the reconciliation of Antony and Caesar can only be temporary, and that it is the result of the threat posed by Pompey. He is rebuked by Antony for expressing this simple but undiplomatic truth. 'Thou art a soldier only. Speak no more.' When Antony has agreed to marry Octavia and the triumvirs have departed, it is left to the cynical soldier with his low opinion of women to show that Antony, despite his marriage, will not abandon Cleopatra. This he does first by describing the Cydnus meeting in extravagantly poetic terms, then by describing how she made defect perfection, and finally in the ultimate tribute to her fascination:

> Age cannot wither her, nor custom stale
> Her infinite variety. Other women cloy
> The appetites they feed, but she makes hungry
> Where most she satisfies.

That the holy priests bless Cleopatra when she is riggish is not more surprising than this eulogy from one of her main critics.

In the next scene in which he appears, Enobarbus again emphasizes that Antony 'will to his Egyptian dish again' and that the marriage to Octavia will be 'the very strangler' of the amity of Antony and Caesar. On this issue he sees more clearly than anyone else in the play. In the scene on Pompey's galley he proposes and supervises the dancing of the Egyptian bacchanals. At the end of the scene, his drunken friendship with Menas, whom we know to be a scoundrel, may be said to exhibit the worst side of his cynical attitude.

In the scene with Agrippa (III.2) the two soldiers ridicule the behaviour of Lepidus; and when Caesar weeps at parting from his sister, Enobarbus implies that tears are unmanly and, in the present case, hypocritical into the bargain. Here he is unjust to Caesar; but his own toughness and cynicism make him ashamed of his own tears later in the play. He is not quite what he pretends to be. In the scenes that follow we watch the vain attempts of Enobarbus to avert Antony's self-destruction and the consequent conflict in his own mind between his affectionate loyalty and his self-interest.

He tries in vain to persuade Cleopatra not to get involved in actual fighting – the war had been declared against her, not against Antony – because Antony, like any soldier, would be distracted by her presence. Enobarbus's aside puts the matter more coarsely. He then tries, equally in vain, to persuade Antony not to fight by sea. This prepares us for the disaster of Actium; but even afterwards Enobarbus decides to 'follow / The wounded chance of Antony, though my reason / Sits in the wind against me'. Cleopatra realizes that by fleeing from the battle she has justified Enobarbus's warnings; but Enobarbus blames Antony only for making 'his will / Lord of his reason'. Every right-thinking person in ancient Rome and Elizabethan London believed that one's life should be governed by reason, and that one's passions should be kept under control. The extent of Antony's deterioration is apparent when he challenges Caesar to single combat; but, despite acknowledgement of his own folly, Enobarbus, the hard-bitten cynic, recognizes the claims of an ideal:

> he that can endure
> To follow with allegiance a fallen lord

> Does conquer him that did his master conquer,
> And earns a place i'th'story.

What makes him change his mind and desert to Caesar is his suspicion that Cleopatra is preparing to make a deal, and still more because of Antony's oscillating moods which indicate the disintegration of his character.

Enobarbus is moved, and ashamed of his own emotion, by Antony's words to his servants. He knows that he is attending his own last party, and he conceals his feelings by criticizing Antony's lack of tact. As soon as he arrives in Caesar's camp he knows that even from the most selfish point of view, he has done ill. His desertion has not been rewarded, as he had expected; and his feelings of regret are made doubly strong by Antony's forgiveness and extraordinary generosity. He condemns himself as a runaway slave and seeks for a ditch in which to die. His repentance earns him a place in the story.

Everyone recognizes that Enobarbus is in some sense a choric figure. He comments on the action and characters in every scene in which he appears, and we are bound to look at both through his eyes, even if we recognize that his perspective is limited, and that it is not always, not necessarily, Shakespeare's own. Apart from this, Enobarbus's last hours are likely to make us revise our previous impressions. There are several times in the course of the play when we are suddenly provided with new insights, and these make us wonder if our previous judgements of characters and actions have been correct.

The Protagonists

When we turn to the character of the protagonists, we find that their actions are diversely judged by their associates and enemies – and this is not merely the inevitable difference between the Roman and Egyptian points of view – as well as by critics, readers and audiences. It looks sometimes as though the critics were writing about different plays; and what makes things even more difficult is that, on several occasions, Shakespeare does not give us clear guidance. This is not because of accidental ambiguities – many of which would be eliminated in rehearsal, both then and now – but because of the real mysteries of human psychology. Every good dramatist must be aware of mixed motives. We do not know for sure – to take a few examples – whether Antony decided to fight at sea because Cleopatra had persuaded him or because Caesar had dared him. We do not know whether his marriage to Octavia is purely one of convenience, which he intends to escape from as soon as it proves an inconvenience. We cannot be certain that Cleopatra is entirely innocent in her conversation with Caesar's envoy; and we cannot be entirely certain that the surrender of the fleet was not by her orders.

Cleopatra admits to feminine cowardice and she is remorseful about her fearful lie which precipitates Antony's suicide; but some of her 'faults' she appears to regard almost as positive qualities of which she has no need to feel ashamed. Antony, in some moods, is more savagely self-critical than even his bitterest critics; in other moods he appears complacent.

Antony

In the first scene Antony loftily denounces Rome and the world of politics and power, proclaiming that mutual love with his wrangling queen is the nobleness of life; but in the next scene the world he has ostensibly rejected demands his attention. The wars of his brother and Fulvia, the continued success of the Parthians, the threat from Pompey and the death of Fulvia – any one of these would compel his departure from Egypt. He is ashamed of his neglect of duty, and instead of calling his love 'the nobleness of life', he now speaks of the 'strong Egyptian fetters' which make him enslaved to sensual pleasure. The woman to whom everything was becoming now seems to him a cunning trickster.

Antony, indeed, is his own severest critic. On several occasions he expresses genuine shame, as when he confesses to Caesar that 'poisoned hours' had bound him up from his own knowledge; or when he tells Octavia (II.3) that he had not kept his square; or when, after his flight from Actium, he says that the land is ashamed to bear him (III.11) and urges his followers to share his treasure and desert. He tells Cleopatra that his sword is made weak by his affection. But his bitterest self-reproach comes at times when he has reason to doubt Cleopatra's fidelity. His love for her then seems to be vicious sensuality:

> The wise gods seal our eyes;
> In our own filth drop our clear judgements: make us
> Adore our errors.

The same contrast between lust and love is expressed in two of Shakespeare's sonnets. In one he had said 'Let me not to the marriage of true minds / Admit impediments'; in the other he had proclaimed that 'Th'expense of spirit in a waste of shame / Is lust in action'. The two sonnets are addressed to different persons: Antony's contradictory estimates of his love both refer to Cleopatra.

When Antony thinks that Cleopatra engineered the surrender of the fleet to Caesar – though it seems merely the last of many desertions for which his own declining fortunes are responsible – he feels he has lost his identity, that it is 'indistinct / As water is in water' (IV.14).

Yet despite his rage at Cleopatra – the flogging of Thidias is a kind of substitute for his violent feeling against her – he is soon pacified. After Actium a single kiss made amends; and after the Thidias episode he is soon satisfied by Cleopatra's assurances of fidelity; and what he had regarded as the final proof of her perfidy is soon overturned by the false story of her death.

Antony's treatment of Octavia lays him open to damaging criticism. He confesses that he has married her for political reasons; and for the same reasons Caesar is willing to put at risk his sister's happiness. Antony decides that he will return to Egypt only twenty lines after promising to turn over a new leaf. But in the scene where he departs from Rome with Octavia he is given two beautiful images describing his bride which show that he – or Shakespeare – appreciates her:

> The April's in her eyes: it is love's spring,
> And these the showers to bring it on . . .
>
> Her tongue will not obey her heart, nor can
> Her heart inform her tongue – the swan's-down feather
> That stands upon the swell at the full of tide,
> And neither way inclines. (III.2)

Yet many critics believe that when Antony tells Octavia (III.4) that Caesar's actions are damaging to his honour, and agrees to her going to Rome to effect a reconciliation, he is really looking for an opportunity to return to Egypt. Octavia sees both sides of the quarrel. She accepts that Antony's honour is precious to him, even though he has a selective attitude to the way his own actions damage it. Later in the play, his dying speech after his bungled suicide is concerned partly with his former glory as 'the greatest prince o' the world', and partly with the fact that he has died honourably rather than surrender:

> Not cowardly put off my helmet to
> My countryman; a Roman, by a Roman
> Valiantly vanquished.

In spite of his jealousy of subordinates who do too well, exacerbated by his own feelings of guilt at having neglected his duties, he retains the loyalty of many of his followers, long after they know he cannot win. We can see why this is so from his farewell to his servants (IV.2), from his treatment of his soldiers (IV.8), and above all from Eros' self-sacrifice to avoid killing his 'dear master', his 'captain', and his emperor, with 'that noble countenance / Wherein the worship of the whole world lies'. After Antony's death, the grief of Caesar and his associates and the laments of Cleopatra leave us with a sense of his magnificence and a willingness to be charitable to his weaknesses. Cleopatra's dream of Antony, though dismissed as fantasy by Dolabella, is of a man transfigured by her love, and by the selectivity of grief, but inevitably it plays a significant part in our final assessment of the hero. So too does Cleopatra's determination to be worthy of him. He appears in the light of 'the consecration and the poet's dream' as a mythological figure not unworthy of Hercules from whom he was descended, and of the Bacchus with whom he was compared.

Cleopatra

Cleopatra is one of Shakespeare's most complex characters, and certainly his most elaborate portrait of a woman. It used to be thought that Shakespeare was drawing on his memories of the Dark Lady of the sonnets, but all Cleopatra's characteristics are outlined by Plutarch, who seems to have been her reluctant admirer. Plutarch's portrait and her legendary reputation were combined in the description of the Cydnus meeting, in which she deliberately assumed the appearance of Venus and thus started rumours that the goddess was come to wed Bacchus. Shakespeare does not begin with this episode: he used it retrospectively after the betrothal of Antony and Octavia when Cleopatra had been absent from the stage long enough for the audience not to make damaging comparisons between this ideal portrait and the less than ideal portrayal by a male actor. (This is not to imply that the actor was anything but brilliant: Shakespeare would not have written the play until he knew he could cast it.)

Cleopatra is introduced to us as a strumpet (a word which is not used precisely as one who sells her favours, but rather as one who is promiscuous). Numerous critics have followed Philo's lead and assured us that she displays all the arts of harlotry, that she is a 'courtesan of genius' (Sidney Lee), a 'Manon Lescaut with a crown on her head' (Duport). But the text does not fully support such a verdict. We first see her as a wrangling queen whom everything becomes, demanding of Antony how much he loves her, teasing him about the messengers from Rome, and about his wife, and then agreeing at the end to wander in disguise through the streets of Alexandria. We are left with Antony's testimonial that in Cleopatra 'every passion fully strives / To make itself . . . fair and admired'.

When she realizes that a Roman thought has struck Antony, Cleopatra is naturally afraid that if he leaves her he may never return. She assumes that attack is the best defence and accuses him of betraying her, of being the greatest liar and, when she hears of Fulvia's death, of being without a heart. She mocks his anger and his pride in being descended from Hercules; then, realizing that she has gone too far, she apologizes and accepts that his honour compels him to leave.

During Antony's absence, Cleopatra expresses her love more openly and directly, by the evocation of his physical presence, by comparison with her former lovers, by memories of their times together and, not least, by her violent attack on the messenger who brings news of his marriage. Although Antony appears a gorgon (for his faithlessness), 'another way he's a Mars'. She is heartened later by the Messenger's diplomatic account of Octavia. Her changing attitude to the Messenger is high comedy; but she is ashamed of her unroyal treatment of him.

Meanwhile, in the scenes in Italy, the fascination of Cleopatra is always before our eyes. There are a dozen references to her, one as long as fifty-six lines, and the choric assurances of Enobarbus that age cannot wither her and that she is blessed by the priests when she is riggish all make it obvious that Antony will eventually return. Cleopatra's conduct in Acts III and IV is controversial and ambiguous. Some believe that the decision to fight at sea was Antony's own; others agree with Canidius and blame Cleopatra. The soldiers are inevitably bitter at her flight from the battle, but it is Antony they chiefly blame. The Thidias scene, as we have already pointed out, is equally a matter of debate. Was she meditating the betrayal of Antony in order to safeguard her position as queen, or merely pretending to do so in order to hoodwink Caesar? It is difficult to believe in her treachery just after her reaction to Antony's words – 'To the boy Caesar send this grizzled head' – and her oath after the episode convinces Antony and most members of an audience. As we have suggested in the previous chapter, her apparent agreement with Thidias that her 'honour was not yielded, but conquered merely' is quietly ironical. Yet G. Wilson Knight speaks of Cleopatra in this scene as possessing 'an utterly selfish streak of bottomless evil', of 'unutterable baseness'.[1] She has decided to betray

Antony and try to win Caesar, as she had won Julius. This interpretation is improbable.

In the scene in which Antony says farewell to his servants, Cleopatra is puzzled and twice asks Enobarbus to interpret. Antony knows, as presumably she does not, that the military situation is hopeless. Yet the two scenes (IV.4, IV.8) where Cleopatra helps to arm Antony and welcome him after his victory as

> Lords of lords!
> O infinite virtue, com'st thou smiling from
> The world's great snare uncaught?

show her at her most inspired and most inspiring.

Although Antony assumes that the surrender of the fleet was Cleopatra's doing and threatens to kill her, she was almost certainly innocent; but, terrified of his rage, she sends word that she has slain herself, realizing too late what the effect will be.

When Antony dies, Cleopatra at once decides on suicide, and is only prevented from stabbing herself by Proculeius's intervention. She sends word to Caesar that she wishes to die: this is because a world without Antony is worthless, because she wishes to be worthy of him by following his example, and because she cannot bear the shame, of which Antony had warned her, of being led in Caesar's triumph. Some critics, indeed, suppose that she would not have committed suicide if she could have escaped that shame, and that the lie about her treasure is a sign that she still hopes to live. But it is apparent from what she says immediately after Caesar's departure that she sees through his assurances and that she had tricked him into believing that she intended to live (see pp. 20 and 30 above). That she died to avoid the ultimate humiliation as well as for love of Antony is hardly surprising. Her motives are mixed. Motives, except in fiction, usually are. One strong motive for living – Caesar's threat to murder her children – does not appear to come into her calculations; but Shakespeare may have decided not to complicate matters by introducing this particular motive.

The suicide is ritualistic, even theatrical. She dies a queen, and she dies also as a bride; she calls Antony husband for the first time. She dies also as the bride of Death. The sexual undertones are apparent in the dialogue with the Clown, in her immortal longings, in her words about the stroke of death 'as a lover's pinch, / Which hurts, and is desired', in her mock anxiety lest Antony should spend his first kiss on Iras, and in the words of her last speech, which welcome death as a form of love. Cleopatra overcomes the fear, the weakness she had admitted; and she is helped in this by her scorn of Caesar, fortune's knave, and of the vile world of policy in which he operates. This is a reversion to Antony's dismissal of imperial Rome in the first scene of the play.

Cleopatra's royalty is stressed in Charmian's farewell tribute (royal, princess, royal kings) but this emphasis is juxtaposed with a phrase that daringly reminds us of her femininity: 'A lass unparalleled'. Charmian also reminds us of the first meeting with Antony, when she was attired like Venus, by addressing her as 'eastern star', that is the planet Venus. To Caesar's horror, she had also been attired as Isis who (as Lucius learns at the end of *The Golden Ass* of Apuleius) is Venus in her local habitat. It has been pointed out that when Isis appears to Lucius she bore a cup of gold 'out of the mouth whereof the serpent Aspis lifted up his head with a swelling throat', and that Proserpine is another manifestation of the goddess. As Harold Fisch says:

Shakespeare presents in the fifth act a ritual of apotheosis in which Antony and Cleopatra . . . put off mortality and announce their union as god and goddess . . . a ritual marriage to be consummated in the afterworld . . . It is an amazing piece of virtuosity, this latter day dramatization of the most primitive and powerful of fertility myths.[2]

But, of course, here and in Cleopatra's dream of Antony, we are left to choose between the feeling that she is deluded, and that she is genuinely inspired.

Although such mythological overtones are important, they should not be allowed to conceal the purely human qualities of the heroine. Cleopatra holds Antony by her infinite variety, and this is not restricted to her talents as a lover. She is a good companion and comrade; she delights in billiards and angling, in dressing up, in wandering the streets in disguise, in practical jokes, in feasting and drinking. She is always role-playing, living up to her various ideas of herself. She knows that woman, no less than man, plays many parts on the stage of life. Like Antony, she earns the loyalty and affection of her servants. Above all, it should be remembered that she develops in the course of the play and that after the death of Antony she reveals qualities which cast a retrospective light on their whole relationship.

It should be mentioned that some critics have complained that the Cleopatra depicted at the beginning of the play is totally incompatible with the Cleopatra of the death scene; that in the first acts she is a courtesan rather than a queen, but that in the last scenes of the play she becomes a thoughtful and motherly woman. Shakespeare, these critics suggest, was following the ordinary Elizabethan method of creating individual scenes, effective in isolation, but involving psychological inconsistency. As J. I. M. Stewart pointed out in *Character and Motive in Shakespeare* such criticism is based on preconceptions about the influence of Elizabethan theatrical practice on Shakespeare and on a curiously limited view of human psychology.[3] It may be added that the idea of a 'motherly' Cleopatra seems to be based on her comparison of the asp to a baby at her breasts.

Charmian and Iras

Granville-Barker calls Charmian and Iras 'worthless trulls', an unkind assessment which he is afterwards compelled to modify. For they both partake of the queen's glory in the final scene. As we have pointed out (p. 45) Cleopatra is on familiar terms with them, and Charmian teases her without being afraid of the threatened reprisals. At the end they both resolve to die with their mistress. Their decision is instinctive, partly from their shared horror of the shame of appearing in Caesar's triumph, and partly from love and loyalty. It is Iras, more docile than her 'wild bedfellow', Charmian, who says, even before Cleopatra has reminded her of the shame:

> Finish, good lady; the bright day is done,
> And we are for the dark.

Cleopatra calls them both 'my noble girls', and Charmian 'noble and kind'. She kisses them farewell, and Iras is the first to die. Charmian survives long enough to speak the Queen's epitaph, to perform the last service to her, and to proclaim the rightness of the suicide. Although she loved long life better than figs, she chooses to shorten her life rather than be dishonoured. Hardly a 'trull'!

Caesar

Antony's rival, Caesar, is contrasted with him in every possible way. He is single-minded in his pursuit of power, as Antony is not; he is self-controlled and abstemious, an indifferent soldier, who relies on his subordinates to bring him victory, lacking in generosity, somewhat priggish, an effective and unscrupulous politician, who uses deceit without any moral qualms. He is introduced to us bitterly criticizing Antony's neglect of his duties and obligations, and deploring his morals. When he does give Antony his due, it is for his past distinction as a soldier. In the same scene Caesar defends his own conduct and attitude; and, in the last act, when he hears of Antony's death, he is still anxious to justify himself:

> Go with me to my tent, where you shall see
> How hardly I was drawn into this war,
> How calm and gentle I proceeded still
> In all my writings. Go with me, and see
> What I can show in this.

He is his own public relations officer. But earlier in the same scene he had admitted that either he or Antony had to be destroyed because there was not room for them both: they 'could not stall together / In the whole world'. It is clear throughout the play that Caesar resents the affection Antony inspires, in spite of his moral defects, and that he feels continually that Antony looks down on him as a 'boy' and as a feeble soldier. After accusing Antony of 'practise' and of breaking his oath, he readily agrees to the marriage of his beloved sister to the man whose morals he had been deploring, so readily indeed that one is prompted to suspect that he originated the proposal. As J. Leeds Barroll puts it:

It is not difficult to respond to this action with the assumption that Caesar is hypocritically laying the basis for the future *casus belli*, for he is offering a valued sister in marriage to an Antony whom, earlier in the play, he had condemned as a profligate . . . it is just as easy to assume opposite possibilities.[4]

It is apparent that Caesar has a genuine love for his sister – it is the only affection he reveals in the course of the play – but he is willing to risk her happiness for political ends. In the scene in which he takes a tearful farewell of Octavia, he shows from his distrust of Antony that he is aware of the risk he is taking:

> Let not the piece of virtue which is set
> Betwixt us as the cement of our love,
> To keep it builded, be the ram to batter
> The fortress of it;

Within a very short time, Caesar sets out to show that he is the dominant partner. He makes a new war against Pompey without consulting Antony and he speaks slightingly of him in public; he dismisses Lepidus from the triumvirate on the improbable grounds that he had become cruel. Antony feels that he himself has been demoted and that his honour is at stake. It almost looks as though Caesar were provoking a quarrel, for which Antony's return to Cleopatra gives him a retrospective justification. He has no difficulty in finding others.

Although the war is officially declared against Egypt, its main purpose is to destroy Antony. Caesar incites Cleopatra to betray her lover and tells Thidias to make lavish promises on his behalf, which he has no intention of honouring. He employs similar tactics later when he tries to persuade Cleopatra of his friendly intentions, but in this case he destroys his credibility by threatening to murder her children.

The terms in which he orders a feast for his victorious soldiers are sufficiently chilling: they have earned a feast and the food would otherwise be wasted. The order is immediately preceded by Antony's invitation to all his 'sad captains' and immediately followed by the touching scene with his servants. The juxtaposition of Caesar's grudging feast shows one difference between the generous and friendly Antony and his mean-spirited rival.

Caesar does, however, show signs of real feeling on two occasions: one, when he parts from his sister, has been noted; the other is when he hears of Antony's death:

> But yet let me lament
> With tears as sovereign as the blood of hearts
> That thou, my brother, my competitor
> In top of all design, my mate in empire,
> Friend and companion in the front of war,
> The arm of mine own body, and the heart
> Where mine his thoughts did kindle . . .

Even here, one cannot help noticing, he is thinking, 'It might have been me'; and he goes on to justify his own acts, and to evade responsibility for the death of Antony.

We are never allowed to get close to Caesar. He never soliloquizes and he is never alone on stage, so we must judge him by his deeds and by his exercises in self-justification. He ends up, as he always intended, as the sole ruler of the empire; but we may well be left agreeing with Cleopatra about the luck of Caesar. We are delighted that he is outwitted by Cleopatra, that the machiavel is revealed as an unpolicied ass, for machiavellian policy implied absolute unscrupulousness.

Lepidus

Little need be said about the other characters. The ineffective and well-meaning Lepidus is developed from the thumb-nail sketch in *Julius Caesar* where he is described as one meet to be sent on errands. He is gulled by Antony on Pompey's galley, where he is made drunk by his inability to say no, and he is splendidly satirized by Enobarbus and Agrippa (III.2). He knows that he is not in the same class as the other triumvirs, and he suspects that he is not fully informed of what is going on.

Dolabella

Dolabella, who betrays Caesar's plans to Cleopatra because of his sympathy with her in her bereavement, is based on a single sentence in Plutarch and a scene in Daniel's play. He is Cleopatra's last, if unintentional, conquest; and his tactful way of puncturing her rhapsodies about Antony – 'Gentle madam, no' – shows him to be the most sensitive of Caesar's entourage.

Pompey

Perhaps the most interesting of the minor characters is Pompey. He tries, not very successfully, to be worthy of his father, and the support he obtains is largely due to his father's name. He professes devotion to the cause for which his father, Brutus, and Cassius had died. But what he really wants is a share of power, and he forgets his principles when he is offered a slice of it in the shape of Sardinia and Sicily. He is not unscrupulous enough to succeed; but his concern is not with morality so much as with reputation. His most revealing remark, as we have seen (p. 33), is made to Menas, who offers to butcher his guests.

4. Interpretations

As we have seen in the previous chapter, critical dissatisfaction with *Antony and Cleopatra* until the present century was partly due to the idea that it was a chronicle history, trammelled by historical facts, and partly due to a vain attempt to divide it into five acts, and to a failure to appreciate that a large number of short scenes could coexist on the Elizabethan stage with a unity of design. (The scene division did not rule out the possibility of one or more intervals.) Labelling the play as a History was an attempt to explain why it lacked the close-knit structure of *Othello* or *Macbeth*. Yet *Othello* has a long gap in its structure while the characters sail from Venice to Cyprus; and *Macbeth* was based on historical fact however much Shakespeare deviated from it when it suited his purposes. Moreover, in dramatizing the better known story of Antony and Cleopatra, he omitted incidents an historian would consider important, he telescoped events, and he departed from the facts when it seemed dramatically useful to do so. The impression he nevertheless gives of reasonable fidelity to history may be because the raw material had already been processed by Plutarch into a biographical masterpiece, and by North into an inaccurate translation which remains one of the glories of Elizabethan prose.

1

Accepting the rightness of the structure used by Shakespeare has not led critics to agree on the interpretation of the play. Some of their conflicting opinions tell us more about their authors than about the play itself. Most critics in the nineteenth century assumed that the play, (whether deliberately or in an indirectly didactic way) warned us of the dire results of neglecting our duty for the sake of extra-marital sexual pleasure. 'Lasciviousness' was the favourite condemnatory word, and Antony a 'sensualist and voluptuary' who 'dragged a fine nature through the common sewer of licentiousness'. Cleopatra was dismissed as a courtesan or harlot, and Antony as a strumpet's fool. Such an attitude to the lovers echoes the Roman point of view as expressed by Philo and Demetrius in the first lines of the play. It was an attitude which fitted with a period which saw the rapid expansion of the British empire – often compared to that of the Roman empire – when there was talk of tribes without the law, and when there was a good deal of hypocrisy with regard to sexual relations.[1] If Octavius Caesar, as depicted by Shakespeare, was an unattractive embodiment of the call of duty, and if the world of politics represented in the play was seedy and corrupt, that only showed the superiority of England,

> Where Freedom broadens slowly down
> From precedent to precedent.

At the opposite end of the scale are the critics who find Cleopatra so enchanting that they write as counsel for the defence, and they cannot consistently blame Antony for sharing their infatuation. Swinburne, indeed, in revolt against Victorian respectability, thought that Cleopatra needed no defence:

Shakespeare has elsewhere given us an ideal incarnation the perfect mother, the perfect daughter, the perfect mistress, or the perfect maiden: here only once for all he has given us the perfect and the everlasting woman.[2]

Although one is left uncertain about which of Shakespeare's women fit into the various categories, Swinburne's point about Cleopatra's femininity is clear enough.

As Maynard Mack has wisely said, those who want clear-cut answers 'should turn to other authors than Shakespeare, and should have been born into some other world than this'.[3] We should therefore be wary of dogmatic assertions by critics who are convinced that they alone hold the key to the correct interpretation of the play.

It is true that moralists and preachers from Antony's time to ours have used his fate to 'point a moral and adorn a tale', in particular the moral that sexual passion often leads to disaster; and, since most moralists are men, the women are usually blamed for leading men astray from the narrow path of duty. Dante encounters Cleopatra and Dido in hell (Canto 5), though not their partners in sin, Antony and Aeneas. This example is given by Franklin B. Dickey in *Not Wisely but Too Well*, and he provides many more examples of classical and medieval condemnations of Antony and Cleopatra.[4] Horace (Epode 9) lamented 'The Roman soldier by a woman tied in slavish bands'. Velleius Paterculus, one of Augustus's officers, not unnaturally declared that Antony's mind was made feeble by his love; Josephus accused Cleopatra of using witchcraft to entrap Antony; Pliny regarded the lovers as 'famous patterns of extravagance and intemperance'; Appian blamed Antony's subservience to Cleopatra which made him do things 'without respect of

God, or of man's law'; Boccaccio declared that Antony's unbridled lust led him into great infamy; and, to give a last of Dickey's examples: 'Spenser twice uses the story of Antony and Cleopatra to exemplify the sins of lust and pride . . . and the feminizing effects of passion'. That Shakespeare was writing in this tradition and that he shared the opinions quoted was the view of Henry Morley. He expressed it neatly in his parody of Dryden's title and sub-title, *All for Love: or the World Well Lost*. Shakespeare, he suggested, might have entitled his *All for Lust: or the World Ill Lost*. This contrasts Shakespearian morality with the decline of moral standards in the age of Dryden. The trouble with Morley's label, and with its endorsement by later critics, is that it appears to conflict with the impression left on us as we leave the theatre after having witnessed Cleopatra's triumphant suicide. Bernard Shaw realized this. In the preface to *Three Plays for Puritans* (a volume which included his *Caesar and Cleopatra*) he declared that Shakespeare gave 'a faithful picture of the soldier broken down by debauchery and the typical wanton in whose arms such men perish'. Then, he complains, Shakespeare 'finally strains all his huge command of rhetoric and stage pathos to give a theatrical sublimity to the wretched end of the business, and to persuade foolish spectators that the world was well lost by the twain'. Shaw's own command of rhetoric was used to distort the facts of the case. The unique Cleopatra cannot justly be described as a typical wanton; and the words used to describe the style of the last act – rhetoric, stage pathos, theatrical sublimity – are derogatory ways of describing great dramatic poetry. Shaw himself, who remained a virgin until the age of thirty, never allowed his sexual adventures to interfere with his political and professional duties, and apparently married for companionship, was unlikely to be sympathetic to the Antonys of the world; but at least he recognized that Shakespeare's attitude at the end of the play was not compatible with puritanical condemnation of the lovers.

One has to remember, as Dickey himself admits, that in Chaucer's poem, *The Legend of Good Women*, Cleopatra figures as one of Love's martyrs; and Shakespeare was as likely to be influenced by his favourite poet as by a whole congregation of moralists. Another poet, Samuel Daniel, as we have seen (p. 19) gives a surprisingly favourable portrait of the heroine, despite the comments of a moralizing chorus.

It was inevitable that with the greater sexual freedom of the post-Victorian world, the critical attitude to *Antony and Cleopatra* underwent a change. Readers of Lawrence, Joyce, Huxley and Greene (to name no others) were less likely to adopt a simple moralistic condemnation of the lovers than nineteenth-century readers had done. An incident such as the abdication crisis showed that it was possible to sympathize with a man who regarded love as a stronger imperative than duty – even if Mrs Simpson was hardly in the same class as Cleopatra.

Yet the conflict between moral and aesthetic attitudes to the play continued. Those readers who were enraptured by some of the greatest poetry in the language felt, if unconsciously, that it justified the lovers and redeemed their vices, as the poetry put into the mouths of Othello and Macbeth prevented us from regarding them as criminals. With those flawed heroes, as with Antony and Cleopatra, Shakespeare acted, we may say, as 'poet for the defence'. So there have been a number of critics who have defended the lovers. Wilson Knight spoke of the play's 'transcendental humanism', of its being 'probably the subtlest and greatest of Shakespeare's plays', of its 'visionary and idealistic optimism', endowing 'man with a supernatural glory'.[5] Although these remarks are counterbalanced by Knight's awareness of the play's realism, his overall interpretation is conveyed by the phrases quoted. Yet in spite of his enthusiastic praise of Cleopatra's combination of diversity and unity, of her embodiment of the characteristics of 'Rosalind, Beatrice, Ophelia, Gertrude, Cressid, Desdemona, Cordelia, and Lady Macbeth' – improbable as this may seem – he has some harsh criticisms of her. She is 'utterly deceitful'; she 'shows the most callous and inhuman cruelty'; 'there is in her a streak of obscene evil'. Unlike most commentators, he thinks that in the Thidias scene she is trying to win Caesar, and that she here displays 'an utterly selfish streak of bottomless evil'.

John Dover Wilson, in his edition of the play, was convinced that it represented Shakespeare's 'hymn to man';[6] and Harold S. Wilson declared that the play

is a vision of love which glorifies man and woman, so that with all their faults . . . they yet rise to tragic dignity, a tragic reconciliation and serenity, compared with which the dreams of earthly empire shrink almost into insignificance: ultimately their love is everything, or all that matters to them and to us.[7]

Robert Speaight, an excellent actor and a devout Christian, went even further. Starting from Knight's idea of transcendental humanism, he concluded his chapter on the play with these words:

It is the most dazzling, even if not the the most profound of Shakespeare's visions, and it would never quite come to him again. Through it he asserts, without either moral censure of romantic compromise, his belief in the resurrection of the flesh.[8]

J. L. Simmons may have been thinking of this passage when he said that 'the grandest irony' of the play 'is that even the member of the audience who approaches it with Christian expectations is forced, finally, to approve the lovers'.[9] This is not strictly true. One has only to peruse the criticism of the last two hundred and fifty years to see that only a small minority have whole-heartedly approved of the lovers. Derek Traversi well described the two ways of looking at the play, whether we should regard it as 'a tragedy of lyrical inspiration, justifying love by presenting it as triumphant over death, or is it rather a remorseless exposure of human frailties, a presentation of spiritual possibilities dissipated through a senseless surrender to passion?'[10] It is, of course, both these things; but the force of the poetry is such that for many people it seems to overwhelm other considerations, or nearly so. L. C. Knights, torn between admiration for the poetry and disapproval of the protagonists, declares that it is

one of the signs of a great writer that he can afford to evoke sympathy or even admiration for what, in his final judgment, is discarded or condemned. In *Antony and Cleopatra* the sense of life's untutored energies is pushed to its limit, and Shakespeare gives the maximum weight to an experience that is finally 'placed'. It is perhaps this that makes the tragedy so sombre in its realism, so little comforting to the imagination.[11]

However that may be, we should remember that the Roman view that Antony has been ruined by his passion for Cleopatra, that he has sacrificed duty to lust – a view which he himself shares when a Roman thought strikes him, or when he suspects Cleopatra of treachery – is not necessarily the poet's. For it is made apparent in the course of the play that the pursuit of power in a fallen world is not obviously morally superior to the pursuit of love, flawed as that love is, that it involves sacrifices of principles and personality, and that to succeed in it, one must stoop to conquer. Hypocrisy and deceit become tactical necessities, any means have to be employed to achieve and retain power, including betrayal, murder, blackmail, and incitement to treachery. When Cleopatra wishes that the asp could speak, so that it could call Caesar 'ass unpolicied', I suppose every member of every audience, whether openly or secretly, rejoices in the defeat of machiavellian policy. One has to remember that Machiavelli was a bogey-man and that Elizabethans and Jacobeans would applaud his defeat, as much as they would agree with the moralists about the dangers of passion.

2

We cannot be certain that Shakespeare, writing within a tradition, was circumscribed by it. He may have written a play in defiance of it. The orthodox view of Coriolanus's treachery was opposed by Machiavelli, and for once Shakespeare's view of the matter approximates to his. Nor can we be sure that Shakespeare's views coincided with those of his sources. Despite the marginal note in North's Plutarch on the Seleucus episode, implying that Cleopatra's performance was designed to deceive Caesar, many critics believe that Shakespeare here deviated from his source.

Is there, then, no more objective way of discovering how we should interpret the play? In this section we shall consider whether an analysis of the imagery can serve that purpose. Caroline Spurgeon believed that, by counting the images and examining the fields from which they are drawn, it is possible to deduce Shakespeare's own conception of the play from the group of images which is numerically predominant.[12] In *Hamlet*, for example, the largest group of images is taken from the field of sickness and medicine: from this Spurgeon deduces that this was a reflection not merely of the sickness of the state of Denmark, but also (more controversially) of the illness of Hamlet himself. Spurgeon has no difficulty in determining that the central group of images in *Antony and Cleopatra*, the one which immediately attracts the attention of the reader, 'consists of images of the world, the ocean and vastness generally'. She goes on to say that 'the dominating note was magnificence and grandeur expressed in many ways, and pictured by continually stimulating our imaginations to see the colossal figure of Antony' – 'demi-Atlas of the earth' – bearing half the world on his shoulders. 'Nothing short of the whole universe suffices for comparison with Antony', Spurgeon declares; 'Not only Cleopatra thinks of him thus; by a common instinct all who know him compare him to great natural phenomena.' She instances Enobarbus's 'mine of bounty' (IV.6.32), Alexas's description of his mood 'Like to the time o'th'year between the extremes' (I.5.51), Lepidus's excuse for his vices, 'the spots of heaven, / More fiery by night's blackness' (I.4.12), and Caesar's obituary: 'The death of Antony / Is not a single doom; in the name lay / A moiety of the world' (V.1.17). The word *world* occurs more than forty times in the course of the play.

Much of the world imagery does indeed relate to Antony, as a few examples may show. In the first scene of the play Antony is called by his critics 'the triple pillar of the world'. He himself tells Cleopatra that in order to estimate his love she 'must needs find out new heaven, new earth' and assures her that 'the wide arch of the ranged empire' is less important than their mutual love. He boasts later that he played as he pleased 'with half the bulk of the world'. When he suspects Cleopatra of treachery, he compares her behaviour to the eclipse of 'our terrene moon', referring both to the actual moon and to Cleopatra in her role as Isis. As Antony lies wounded, one of his guards cries 'The star is fallen'. Cleopatra asks the sun to 'Burn the great sphere thou mov'st in!' After his death, she uses the sun and moon, earth and ocean to describe her dead hero:

> His face was as the heavens, and therein stuck
> A sun and moon, which kept their course and lighted
> The little O o'th'earth.

> His legs bestrid the ocean; his reared arm
> Crested the world;

Caesar, hearing of his death, says that

> The round world
> Should have shook lions into civil streets
> And citizens to their dens.

Shakespeare was remembering the portents that preceded the assassination of Julius Caesar. It is clear that one effect of the cosmic imagery is to elevate Antony into superhuman status – and comparisons with Hercules and Bacchus have a similar effect. But the imagery has another function: it underlines the stakes for which Antony and Caesar are playing, and the world power which Antony is sacrificing because of his love.

Apart from the fact that iterative imagery can often be interpreted in more than one way, Spurgeon's method has been criticized on several other grounds: the categories into which she divides the images are not necessarily the most suitable; she lumps together derivative and original images; and, more seriously, by concentrating on a single iterative image because of its frequency, she tended to oversimplify the plays with which she dealt. The man in ill-fitting garments which recurs several times in *Macbeth* is only one of several groups of images which ought to be taken into consideration; and likewise there are several groups in *King Lear* which are as significant as the image of the tortured body on which Spurgeon concentrated. So in *Antony and Cleopatra* there are several groups of images besides the cosmic imagery already discussed.

One such group is concerned with feeding. As Maurice Charney suggests, images of eating and drinking are used to characterize Egypt as a place of sensual pleasure.[13] This is doubtless true; but as in *Troilus and Cressida*, where eating imagery is predominant, it underlines the fact that the love of Antony and Cleopatra is based on a natural appetite which, like any other, can be indulged to excess. Cleopatra, speaking of her relationship with Julius Caesar, says that then, in her salad days when she 'was green in judgement', she was 'a morsel for a monarch'. A similar expression is used by Antony in his jealous rage:

> I found you as a morsel cold upon
> Dead Caesar's trencher. Nay, you were a fragment
> Of Gnaeus Pompey's.

Troilus complains similarly that the unfaithful Cressida is giving to Diomed 'the fragments, scraps, the bits and greasy relics' collected from the dirty plates after a meal.

In Act II we are told that Antony 'sits at dinner' – a phrase used with a sexual connotation – and Pompey, not wishing him to return to Rome, hopes that 'Epicurean cooks' will 'sharpen with cloyless sauce his appetite', an epithet which looks forward to what Enobarbus says of Cleopatra:

> other women cloy
> The appetites they feed; but she makes hungry
> Where most she satisfies.

Pompey calls Antony 'this amorous surfeiter'. At his first meeting with Cleopatra, Enobarbus tells his listeners, Antony paid with his heart 'what his eyes eat only', and he prophecies that Antony, despite his marriage to Octavia, 'will to his Egyptian dish again'. At the end of Act III, Enobarbus widens the significance of the eating imagery, when he says that

> when valour preys on reason
> It eats the sword it fights with.

In the last act, the countryman who brings the asps to Cleopatra tells her that 'a woman is a dish for the gods if the devil dress her not' – reminding us that she was a morsel for a monarch, a fragment of Pompey's and Antony's Egyptian dish. She is to be 'eaten' by the asp; and, contemplating suicide, she declares that

> it is great
> To do that thing that ends all other deeds,
> Which shackles accident and bolts up change,

> Which sleeps, and never palates more the dung,
> The beggar's nurse and Caesar's.

In the food imagery, as with the cosmic imagery, there is a certain ambivalence. It is used to emphasize the force of the sexual instinct, and sometimes to degrade love to what Iago calls 'a lust of the blood and a permission of the will'. But after Antony's death, as Charney points out;

The sensual theme is reversed, as Cleopatra prepares for death ... 'Temperance' is a specifically Roman virtue that Antony had earlier denied to Cleopatra: 'I am sure, Though you can guess what temperance should be You know not what it is' (III.12.120) ... Cleopatra ends by forswearing the mortal longings of the senses and negating the quality of Egypt ... The final movement in the imagery of food and drink is toward a Roman temperance.[14]

Against this, it should be remembered that Cleopatra is afraid – or pretends to be afraid – that Antony will 'spend' his first post-mortem kiss on Iras, that her own death is regarded by her almost as a sexual consummation and that Enobarbus had earlier told Antony, 'I do not think there is mettle in death, which commits some loving act upon her, she hath such a celerity in dying' ('dying' in the seventeenth century was regularly used as a synonym for orgasm). Cleopatra, then, is romanized to some extent, but she retains to the end her essential sensuousness.

The sense of conflict and violent movement in the play is partly caused by the wars and rumours of wars from the first scene to the last, and partly by the frequent changes of location and the travelling necessitated thereby – from Egypt to Rome, from Rome to Athens, from Athens to Egypt, and from Egypt to Parthia. But it is reinforced by the imagery and by the use of forceful verbs. Cleopatra says that a Roman thought has *struck* Antony. Antony resolves to *break* his 'strong Egyptian fetters', as though he were a shackled prisoner. Referring to Fulvia's death, he speaks of the way 'our contempts doth often *hurl* from us' and how the hand could 'pluck her back that *shoved* her on'. He says that the people begin to *throw* the dignities of Pompey the Great on his son. Caesar complains alliteratively that Antony '*tumbles* on the bed of Ptolemy', '*reels* the streets at noon' and 'stands the *buffet* with knaves that smell of sweat'. Cleopatra does not describe herself as sunburned, but black with Phoebus' 'amorous pinches', those pinches which, she later tells us, 'hurt and are desired'. She proposes to *pluck* his tidings from Alexas. Lepidus, urging Antony to be diplomatic, asks him to not allow a leaner action to *rend* them. The oars which propelled Cleopatra's barge on the river Cydnus *beat* the water; and 'a strange invisible perfume *hits* the sense of the adjacent wharfs'. Cleopatra urges the messenger to *ram* his tidings in her ears. Enobarbus prophecies that the band that seems to tie Antony and Caesar together 'will be the very strangler of their amity'; and Caesar, fearing the same result, urges Antony not to let the marriage be 'the *ram* to *batter* the fortress' of their love. Eros tells Antony after the battle of Actium that 'death will *seize* Cleopatra'. Antony's generosity *blows* the heart of Enobarbus, who wishes to *throw* his heart 'Against the flint and hardness of his fault'. In the last act, Dolabella is *smitten* to the very heart by Cleopatra's grief for Antony, and she tells Caesar that her wounding shame *smites* her beneath her fall. Caesar in his concluding speech declares that such high events as the death of Antony and Cleopatra '*strike* those that make them'.

Apart from this extraordinary vocabulary of violence, there is plenty of violent action. Cleopatra physically assaults the messenger who brings the news of Antony's marriage to Octavia; she is restrained from treating Seleucus in the same way, and she twice draws a knife.

There are a number of images which were suggested by the overflowing of the Nile, and some by the ebbing and flowing tide. The former help to create the atmosphere of Egypt in contrast to that of Rome, so that we absorb unconsciously the difference between the two ways of life. We hear of the overflowing of Antony's dotage, and that Iras's palm presages chastity as the 'o'erflowing Nile presageth famine'. We are later told by Antony that the Egyptian harvest depends on the flooding:

> The higher Nilus swells,
> The more it promises: as it ebbs, the seedsman
> Upon the slime and ooze scatters his grain
> And shortly comes to harvest.

Earlier Antony had sworn by 'the fire that quickens Nilus' slime'.

There are two striking images relating to things floating on the stream at turn of tide. One expresses Caesar's patrician scorn of the common people:

> This common body,
> Like to a vagabond flag upon the stream,
> Goes to and back, lackeying the varying tide,
> To rot itself with motion.

Antony uses a similar image in his tender comment on Octavia's difficulty in speaking on account of her conflicting emotions:

> Her tongue will not obey her heart, nor can
> Her heart inform her tongue, the swan's-down feather
> That stands upon the swell at full of tide
> And neither way inclines.

More significant are the images relating to melting, and these also bring out the difference between Egypt and Rome. In the first of them Antony proclaims his valuation of Cleopatra, compared with the empire. 'Let Rome in Tiber melt!' Cleopatra in Act II (perhaps remembering this) cries 'Melt Egypt into Nile!' Sometimes the melting is associated with flattery, as so often in Shakespeare.[15] When Antony reproaches Cleopatra for flattering Caesar by mingling eyes with a mere valet, she replies:

> As it determines, so
> Dissolve my life! The next Caesarion smite!
> Till by degrees the memory of my womb,
> Together with my brave Egyptians all,
> By the discandying of this pelleted storm,
> Lie graveless, till the flies and gnats of Nile
> Have buried them for prey!

Later, in the next act, Antony introduces the third factor in the image-cluster, as it is called; dogs, linked to the previous speech by *melt* and *discandy*:

> The hearts
> That spanielled me at heels, to whom I gave
> Their wishes, do discandy, melt their sweets
> On blossoming Caesar.

To blame his followers for deserting him is quite unlike his magnanimity to Enobarbus and others. It may be due to a passage in Plutarch's *Life* of Antony – to which Shakespeare does not otherwise refer – where Antony is compared to Timon, who exiled himself because of the ingratitude of the Athenians. It may be noted in this connection that the image cluster of flatterers-dogs-sweets is the iterative image of *Timon of Athens*, written not long before *Antony and Cleopatra*.

In the next scene, Antony, losing his identity because of his belief that Cleopatra has betrayed him, compares himself to a melting cloud:

> even with a thought
> The rack dislimns, and makes it indistinct
> As water is in water . . .
> Here I am Antony
> Yet cannot hold this visible shape.

When he dies, Cleopatra cries that 'The crown of the earth doth melt'; and, as she herself dies, becoming, as she claims, all air and fire,

Charmian prays the thick cloud to dissolve and rain, 'that I may say /
The gods themselves do weep'. The dissolution of the world of power,
one might say, is paralleled with the dissolving of life itself.

I have discussed elsewhere [16] the repetition of the idea of fortune in
the play. In accordance with recent practice in discussions of imagery
and symbolism, the repetition of ideas and words may also be of considerable significance. Many of the references to fortune are contained,
as one might expect, in the two scenes in which the Soothsayer appears.
He prophecies obscurely what will eventually happen, and warns Antony
that Caesar will be as fortunate in life as he is at games. On several
occasions it is pointed out that ill fortune is due to a failure to seize
opportunities, as when Menas tells Enobarbus that Pompey, the inept
politician, 'doth this day laugh away his fortune', or later comments on
Pompey's refusal to give him permission to murder Caesar and Antony:
'I'll never follow thy palled fortunes more'. So, after the battle of
Actium, Canidius blames Antony that their 'fortune on the sea is out of
breath'. Antony boasts that once he could make and mar fortunes, but
that he now serves fortune when she is adverse. His ambassador salutes
Caesar as 'Lord of his fortunes' and takes his leave with the ambiguous
words: 'Fortune pursue thee'. Caesar can take it as a wish that he would
continue fortunate; but the audience may feel that to be pursued by
fortune makes him a victim. Enobarbus, seeing Antony's increasing
inability to face reality, remarks that 'men's judgements are / A parcel of
their fortunes', implying that the worse one's fortune, the worse one's
judgement will be. Thidias tempts Cleopatra by assuring her that Caesar
would like her to make a staff of his fortunes. Antony, making ready for
his last battle, proposes to brave fortune; and, on hearing of Enobarbus's
desertion, he laments that his fortunes have corrupted honest men – not
here acknowledging that his own defects and mistakes had anything to
do with the desertions from his army. Scarus says that Antony's fortunes
are 'fretted'; and, after the surrender of his fleet, Antony says farewell to
what slender hopes he still clung to, declaring that he and fortune part,
'even here / Do we shake hands'. Cleopatra hopes that by her railing she
may induce the 'false housewife, Fortune' to break her wheel; and this
reference to the wheel of fortune is reinforced by Antony's dying words
about his former fortunes, when he was at the top of the wheel, 'Wherein
I lived; the greatest prince o'th'world'.

Cleopatra in the last scene speaks scornfully of the successful Caesar:

> 'Tis paltry to be Caesar:
> Not being Fortune, he's but Fortune's knave.

She later speaks of herself, with covert irony, as 'his fortune's vassal'; and, finally, as she prepares for death, she imagines that she hears Antony mock 'The luck of Caesar, which the gods give men / To excuse their after wrath'; and she wishes the asp could speak, 'That I might hear thee call great Caesar ass / Unpolicied!'

From one point of view, therefore, we watch the operations of the wheel of fortune, bringing Antony down from greatness to ruin, but these are presented not without irony since Antony is the real architect of his own destruction.[17] Yet, as Caesar recognizes at the end, either he or Antony had to be destroyed. From another point of view, we watch Antony and Cleopatra emancipating themselves from worldly success, and in their defeat scorning the fortunate Caesar. Is their final attitude backed by the poet or did he regard it as a case of sour grapes?

There are some seventy references in the play to honour and nobility, and others to royalty. Sometimes 'honour', as often in Shakespeare, means little more than reputation, rather than the character and behaviour on which reputation should be based. When Ulysses in *Troilus and Cressida* urges Achilles to 'keep honour bright', he merely means that he is losing his reputation as a warrior by his continued inaction. In this play Pompey tells Menas that as he puts honour or reputation before self-interest, he can't agree to the murder of his guests. Even with Antony, though most of the references concern his genuine honour and nobility as well as his reputation, there are some which express his shame for his actions. After Actium, for example, he confesses: 'I have offended reputation, A most unnoble swerving'; 'See,' he continues,

> How I convey my shame out of thine eyes,
> By looking back what I have left behind,
> 'Stroyed in dishonour.

Earlier, faced with Caesar's legitimate complaints, Antony is obviously uneasy:

> The honour is sacred which he talks on now,
> Supposing that I lacked it.

Before long he has to admit that he neglected to keep his sworn agreement because of his 'poisoned hours' in Egypt. His annoyance when his subordinates are too successful, thereby showing up his own inactivity, and his suggestion that in revenge for his own treatment of Thidias, Caesar should 'whip, or hang or torture' Hipparchus, are two examples of his ignoble conduct. More ambiguous is the way he speaks of the threat to his honour from things Caesar has said and done. He tells Octavia: 'If I lose my honour, I lose myself'. We cannot be certain that his encouragement of her visit to her brother is not so that he can take the opportunity of escaping to Egypt.

In the concluding scenes of the play, the word 'noble' seems to be used without irony. Antony calls Eros, who commits suicide rather than kill his master, 'thrice nobler than' himself; and in his last speech he claims that he was once 'the noblest prince of the world'. This self-praise is confirmed by what Eros had said just before of 'that noble countenance / Wherein the worship of the whole world lies'. Cleopatra likewise calls him 'noblest of men' and calls her projected suicide 'what's brave, what's noble'. In the last scene she speaks again of being noble to herself, and of her suicide as a noble deed. This nobility, as we have noted, is associated with her royalty. Iras calls her 'royal Egypt' and 'royal queen'; and Cleopatra reciprocates by calling Charmian noble. Charmian in turn closes her mistress's eyes with the words

> And golden Phoebus never be beheld
> Of eyes again so royal!

and tells the guard that the deed is

> fitting for a princess
> Descended of so many royal kings.

Even Caesar is constrained to admit that Cleopatra 'being royal / Took her own way'.

We have already called attention to the way in which the status of the protagonists is enhanced by their association with divine personages: Antony is descended from Hercules and compared to Bacchus; Cleopatra is compared to Venus – superior, indeed, to artistic representations of Venus – and she dresses as Isis, if indeed she is not the incarnation of the goddess.

Enough has been said to indicate that the imagery cannot be used to decide between conflicting interpretations of the play. Whereas the sickness imagery of *Hamlet*, though it is sometimes misinterpreted, is really unambiguous; and though no one seriously questions the way in which one should interpret the complex imagery of *King Lear*, no such certainty attaches to the significance of the imagery of *Antony and Cleopatra*. It throws a great deal of light on the play, but the light is fitful and ambivalent.

3

We seem to be back at square one, with irreconcilable interpretations of the play. But several modern critics have tried to bridge the gulf between the All-for-Love and the All-for-Lust interpreters. One of them is John Danby who, in an essay reprinted in *Elizabethan and Jacobean Poets*,[18] speaks of 'a peculiarly Shakespearian dialectic' in the play. By this he means that we are presented throughout the play with opposites – Rome and Egypt, the world and the flesh. The constant pattern 'is that of open conflict alternating with diseased truce' – what we have learned to call cold war. To Danby, Caesar is 'the perfect commissar, invulnerable as no human being should be'. His hope of 'universal peace' is as much a delusion as the belief of the lovers that they will meet in an afterworld. Danby argues that in the last two acts of the play Antony and Cleopatra are regarded by Shakespeare and by the audience as 'unhappy and be-dizened and sordid, streaked with the mean, the ignoble, the contemptible'.

Apart from this verdict, with which many will disagree, there is a technical objection: the use of the word 'dialectic' implies that the thesis (the pleasures of Egypt), and the antithesis (the values of Rome) will be followed by a synthesis. But Danby assumes that no synthesis is possible.[19]

Another attempt to bridge the gulf was made by Ernest Schanzer, whose book, *The Problem Plays of Shakespeare*, appeared in 1963, and included a discussion of two other plays, *Julius Caesar* and *Measure for Measure*.[20] A problem play may be defined as one in which there is a moral problem at its centre, and one in which the audience is left with unanswered questions and conflicting impressions. Schanzer excludes two plays often labelled in this way – *All's Well that Ends Well* and *Troilus and Cressida* – because we are not left in 'any real uncertainty in our moral bearings'. But there are surely a number of Shakespeare's plays which leave us with conflicting impressions and unanswered questions, and one may doubt whether *Antony and Cleopatra* should be singled out in this way. In recent years there have been many of Shakespeare's plays which have evoked a mixed response; and once the possibility of sub-text is allowed – hints below the surface of the dialogue – there are bound to be violent disagreements about the interpretation. Should Hamlet kill Claudius? Is Shylock grievously wronged? Is *King Lear*, as Kott thought, Shakespeare's *Endgame*? Was Iago in love with Othello?

Although we may dissent from Schanzer's labelling of *Antony and*

Cleopatra, he himself dissented strongly from Danby's essay, much as he admired it in some ways. He questioned Danby's assumption that Shakespeare was exhibiting Cleopatra's delusions in Act V. Danby had said that 'Shakespeare may have his plays in which "redemption" is a theme ... but Antony and Cleopatra is not one of them'. Schanzer comments:

> I do not find it possible to follow him in this view. If the desolation that begins to make a better life for Cleopatra does not take her away from the flesh-pots, if she does not undergo an ennoblement (if we prefer to confine the word 'redemption' to religious contexts) which carries with it an increase in human kindness and a diminution of selfishness and pride ... it is difficult to see what Shakespeare was doing in the last act.

Professor Anne Barton (in her inaugural lecture at Bedford College, London) went further and argued convincingly that the final act of the play compels us to look at the previous action with new eyes, so that the whole meaning undergoes a transformation. For Cleopatra's suicide does not merely prove her love for Antony after his death; it retrospectively validates her love for him in the past, and in so doing makes Antony's love for her something more than a licentious shirking of his duties as a world ruler. Professor Muriel Bradbrook, on the other hand, regards the last scene as 'the triumph of the dream over the representative of the world', and she speaks of the love of the protagonists as 'mutual fantasy'. This, too, is a possible interpretation, but it is not the only one.

The Elizabethans had several theories of tragedy, and *Antony and Cleopatra* seems curiously to embody them all. First, there is the medieval idea, as expressed in 'The Monk's Tale' in Chaucer's *Canterbury Tales*, that tragedy is concerned with the fall of illustrious men from 'high degree' into misery, and ending wretchedly. The same conception was apparent in the dreary, but immensely popular, *Mirror for Magistrates* (which Shakespeare knew well). In most of the stories there were warnings against the misuse of power, which led to the fall of the rulers, but in some, such as the lament of Cordila, which contributed some phrases to *King Lear*, those who fall are innocent of wrong-doing, and here the message is the inevitable turning of the wheel of fortune, which brings down people in high estate. *Antony and Cleopatra* can be regarded as a tragedy of this kind: Antony, the triple pillar of the world, and Queen Cleopatra are brought to ruin and death.

The second conception of tragedy, based largely on Seneca's plays, and expounded by Sir Philip Sidney in his *Defence of Poesy* is that it should expose the ulcers which are covered with tissue, reveal hidden sins in individuals or society, and make kings fear to be tyrants. Shakespeare was not so directly didactic: his didacticism consisted rather in truth-telling, in holding a mirror up to human nature, in order to demonstrate the results of certain actions. If by returning to an adulterous relationship, you betray your lawful wedded wife, mortally offend your brother-in-law, and neglect your duty to your country, the catastrophic results are predictable.

A third conception of tragedy, apparent in a number of Elizabethan plays although not discussed by critics of the period, is when the hero is confronted with a choice between two principles, both apparently good. In revenge tragedy, for example, the opposing principles may be filial duty on the one hand, and the Christian duty of forgiveness on the other. In *Antony and Cleopatra* they may be love and power, but such a choice may be represented as lust and duty.

Such a conception may be connected with the theory, evolved in later years, that the hero suffers from a fatal flaw which brings about his ruin. In a speech in the first act of Hamlet, cut in the revised version printed in 1623, the hero speaks of the way a small defect in a man's character, sometimes hereditary or a matter of chance, will counteract his 'infinite' virtues. Hamlet is actually speaking about a man's reputation, although critics have extended the meaning to include tragic failure. In some of Shakespeare's heroes this flaw is easily diagnosed: pride in Coriolanus, ambition in Macbeth. It is possible to argue that Antony's fatal defect is either that he allows himself to be governed by passion, or else that he still hankers after the power which his actions have put beyond his reach.

All these theories of Shakespearian tragedy have been applied to *Antony and Cleopatra* by one critic or another; but they all seem to evade the problem posed by audience reaction to the miraculous last scene. Act IV ends the tragedy of Antony; Act V consists of his rehabilitation through the validation of his love by Cleopatra's glorification of it, sealed by her triumphant suicide. Audiences at *Macbeth*, whatever sympathy they may retain for the hero, accept the necessity of his overthrow; audiences at *Hamlet* experience the woe and wonder demanded by Horatio; but at performances of *Antony and Cleopatra*, audiences are swept away by the sheer perfection of the poetry and rejoice that Cleopatra has foiled Caesar, that the personal has overcome the political.

A number of critics have suggested that Shakespeare was already moving towards the tragi-comedies of his last period. Schanzer quotes Bradley's statement that the death of Cleopatra 'is greeted by the reader with sympathy and admiration', Dover Wilson's concurrence that it 'fills us with exultation and delight', and F. P. Wilson's agreement that it is a triumph. Schanzer concludes that this means that our emotional experience resembles that at the end of *Cymbeline* or *The Winter's Tale* rather than that at the end of *Othello* or *King Lear*. The pitiful tragedy of Antony in Act IV, the tragedy of a man who has lost in the power struggle, and apparently lost also in his love, is succeeded by the posthumous transformation of that love in the last act. That the lovers look forward to a reunion in the Elysian fields, and that this may be a delusion, hardly matters, since in a pagan world an after-life was a dreary second best. Only if we think that the lovers are deluded about each other and that they cast a romantic and unreal glamour over their love, does the final scene become a painful exposure of their delusion, rather than a triumphant one. The quality of the poetry cries out against such a judgement.

One other point needs to be made. Caesar declares that the time of universal peace is near, and we are not to think of this as a delusion. Shakespeare was fully aware of the belief that the short interval between wars was a necessary condition for the nativity of Jesus. He was dramatizing the final stages of the pagan world; and in *Cymbeline*, in whose reign Jesus was born, he concluded the play with peace between Britain and Rome, forgiveness of enemies, and reconciliation in the personal sphere.

5. Commentary

Act I

Scene 1

The scene opens, as all Shakespeare's tragedies do (except *Othello*) with minor characters, preparing the way for the entrance of the protagonists; but unlike the openings of *Hamlet*, *King Lear* and *Macbeth*, in this case we are given a scathing denunciation of Antony from the Roman point of view. This consists partly of moral disapproval of his sexual infatuation – the way his adulterous association with Cleopatra interferes with his duties as a world ruler – and is due partly to the insult to Caesar implied by his casual attitude ('Is Caesar with Antonius prized so slight?'). But it derives mostly from disappointment at the fall from greatness, both as a soldier and statesman, of a man both speakers had admired. Demetrius has just arrived from Rome (cf. I.4.7) and he is being informed by Philo, a disgruntled member of Antony's entourage. The first word of the play shows that it begins in the middle of the conversation between the two men. The first short scene between the lovers is thus framed by the criticisms of Philo and Demetrius, which continue after the departure of the lovers. We assume, at first, that they are acting as a kind of chorus, expressing the poet's own views. The audience is bound to be swayed by the forceful opening speeches, however much these initial reactions are modified later; and many critics believe that Shakespeare would not open a play with the expression of opinions which are afterwards falsified or overturned. Yet this is precisely what happens in *Othello* (where Iago's comments on Othello are soon proved to be false) and in *Julius Caesar*.

There is, perhaps, an element of racial prejudice in the opening speeches, in such phrases as 'tawny front' and 'gipsy's lust'. The Egyptian royal family was of Greek origin, and Cleopatra was the first of the Ptolemies who spoke Egyptian. Shakespeare, whether he was aware of this or not, was expressing accurately the official Roman view, shared by Virgil and Horace, on the degeneracy and effeminacy of the near East. This official disapproval was mingled with a good deal of fascination. They knew that Julius Caesar and one of Pompey the Great's sons had fallen for Cleopatra before she met Antony, and Caesar had brought her to Rome as his mistress. (Shakespeare refrains from mentioning this, either in this play or in *Julius Caesar*, where it would have been distracting.)

When the lovers appear, heralded by trumpets and fanned by eunuchs, it is apparent that there is nothing secretive about the relationship, but some recent productions have made the mistake of having the lovers enjoy the publicity. Their conversation is intimate, and not designed to impress or titillate the onlookers. Our moral certainties are likely to receive a jolt, for the lovers are not behaving as we have been led by Philo and Demetrius to expect. The obvious devotion they exhibit, Cleopatra's teasing of Antony, and his echo of Revelation 21.1 in the line, 'Then must thou needs find out new heaven, new earth', convey a favourable impression of their love. (Shakespeare cheerfully indulges in anachronism for he knew that the Book of Revelation was written many years later.)

If the actress lives up to her role – and we must not forget that there were no actresses in Shakespeare's day – we shall be tempted to echo Antony's tribute to the wrangling queen,

> Whom everything becomes – to chide, to laugh,
> To weep; whose every passion fully strives
> To make itself, in thee, fair and admired.

Antony's dismissal of the glories of empire and of the pursuit of power which they involve, his insistence that the real nobleness of life lies in mutual love, cannot easily be dismissed as the delusions of a strumpet's fool. But it should be noted that before the end of the act Antony does not wholly believe in his own declaration that kingdoms are clay.

As the editor of the Penguin edition notes, 'To do thus' (36) may be a general statement of love, or may be accompanied by an embrace or a kiss. Some years ago Nugent Monck, the theatre director, assured a Shakespeare conference at Stratford-upon-Avon that a kiss, except possibly on the hand, was out of the question because of the voluminous farthingale which kept men at a discreet distance. Yet it is by no means certain that Cleopatra was dressed like Elizabeth I and probable that she and the Roman Octavia were dressed differently. In any case the obstacle of a farthingale was not as serious as the big drum over which Professor Cusins kisses Major Barbara in Shaw's play, as a delegate who had performed this feat pointed out.

Cleopatra's four references to Fulvia, Antony's wife, remind us that their love is adulterous, though it is not till much later that we learn that Cleopatra too was married.

Antony's final proposal, derived from Plutarch's account, that he and his royal mistress should wander in disguise through the streets and note the qualities of people, though shocking to the Roman ideal of *gravitas* seems singularly innocent and rather endearing. One is reminded of the attack in the first scene of *The Merchant of Venice* on those who put on an act of 'wisdom, gravity, profound conceit'. Shakespeare, however, suppresses the fact that Antony in his disguise sometimes received mocks and blows.

Scene 2

The first part of this scene (1–79) has two main purposes: to reveal the atmosphere of the Egyptian, and to hint at the tragic conclusion of the play. Literate members of the audience would know the main outlines of the story and of Cleopatra's suicide after Antony's death, but the fortune–telling is a useful reminder to the Globe patrons, that all will not end well. (The play may also have been staged at the Blackfriars when it became available to Shakespeare's company, but this would be after the first performance.)

The stage direction at the beginning of the scene introduces four characters (Lamprius, Rannius, Lucillius and Mardian) who do not speak, and only the last of them appears later in the play. (The Penguin edition omits these characters.) Possibly Shakespeare changed his mind after writing the entry, deciding that it was preferable to have a more intimate scene; but as both the Soothsayer and Enobarbus, mentioned also in the initial stage direction, do not enter until later in the scene (6, 11), I believe that the Romans should enter with Enobarbus to take part in the banquet, even though they are given no words to say. Enobarbus, too, has nothing to say while the fortune-telling is proceeding, except 'Mine, and most of our fortunes, tonight, shall be drunk to bed'. It is plainly easier for him to say this if there are other revellers present besides Charmian, Iras and Alexas.

The conversation between the women, the Soothsayer and Alexas, with its sexual innuendos and its jests about cuckoldry, is no more indecent than that of the gentlemen in *Romeo and Juliet* or that of the ladies in *Love's Labour's Lost*, but in its context it can give the impression that the sexual morals of Cleopatra's court are somewhat lax. Yet it should be observed that Charmian wants husbands, rather than a succession of casual lovers, and many children rather than barren relationships.

The Soothsayer's prophecies are not precisely fulfilled. Charmian does

70

outlive her mistress by a minute or two, long enough to speak her epitaph, but Iras does not, so that their fortunes are not quite identical.

It was dramatically important to introduce the Soothsayer early in the play, as he has an important interview with Antony in the third scene of Act II.

The remainder of the scene (81–198) shows the cumulative pressures on Antony to leave Egypt. First, Fulvia's wars against Antony's brother, and then with his brother against Caesar. These facts, taken, as we have seen, from Appian's *Civil Wars*, are left obscure, presumably because Shakespeare thought that the details were of no dramatic importance. Secondly, the military successes of Labienus make Antony ashamed of his own inactivity. He resolves to break his Egyptian fetters – as Daniel calls them. Thirdly comes the news of Fulvia's death. Fourthly, there are the naval successes of Pompey, which involve Antony's obligations as a member of the triumvirate. He is therefore driven by a variety of motives – his sense of shame, political expediency, his promises, and the necessity of settling his wife's affairs – to break with the 'enchanting' queen. By this word he meant not merely her fascination, but also the spells she had apparently used to entrap him.

In the dialogue that follows it is the cynical Enobarbus who bears witness to the attractiveness of Cleopatra, at the same time as he admits she is a consummate actress. It is Antony who attacks her character and wishes he had never seen her. He realizes that he will find it difficult to escape from her toils, unless he brings himself to think the worst of her. This dialogue is in prose, suitable for Enobarbus's bawdy comments, but it reverts to verse at the end of the scene when Antony explains why he must leave Egypt. However, the fact that he is going to ask Cleopatra's permission is sufficient indication that the break is not likely to be as permanent as he had apparently resolved only a few minutes before.

Scene 3

Cleopatra, aware that a Roman thought has struck Antony (I.2.84), but ignorant of its nature, outlines her strategy for retaining his allegiance: she had told Alexas to report her mood as contrary to Antony's, whatever that happens to be. Charmian says, 'if you did love him dearly, / You do not hold the method to enforce / The like from him' and that Cleopatra ought to cross him in nothing. She retorts that this is the way to lose him; and in the scene which follows she carries out her proposed strategy. Her attacks on Antony, since we have been warned of them beforehand, are comic in their effect. She accuses him of dissembling, but we know that she is the real dissembler. At this stage in their relationship it appears that Antony, despite his determination to leave Egypt, is more completely in love than Cleopatra. We are reminded of Charmian's doubts: '*if* you did love him dearly'. Antony's desertion of Fulvia is taken to be a proof of his lack of constancy; and when he reveals that she is dead, his failure to mourn her makes Cleopatra profess to believe that he will be equally unmoved by her death. The repetition of 'I see' and the rhyming couplet underline the theatrical nature of her indignation. In fact, as we know from Antony's soliloquy in the previous scene (119–24), he had belatedly regretted his wife's death.

Cleopatra's most effective hit is to call Antony 'this Herculean Roman'; for, as we have seen, he was proud of his descent from Hercules. Indeed, she realizes that she has gone too far and tries to make amends by a sudden change of tone. Even here she cannot resist calling her forgetfulness 'a very Antony'; and we don't know whether she has really forgotten what she wanted to say, or pretended to forget, so that she could make this crack about Antony. In her last speech she apologizes and accepts the necessity of his departure. She alludes to Antony's declaration in the first scene that 'every thing becomes her'; now she says that if her 'becomings' do not please him, they are damaging to her: they 'kill' her.

The scene is rounded off with a couplet. Shakespeare regarded the first three scenes as unified by the Egyptian setting as well as by the action which is focused on the conflict between love and duty. Although Cleopatra has failed to prevent Antony's departure and she knows very well the pressures that may prevent his return, Antony has not made the definite break with her he seems to have intended; and he swears that he leaves Egypt as her servant and 'making peace or war' as she chooses. This is perhaps an indication that Cleopatra's relationship with Antony, as in the past with Julius Caesar and Gnaeus Pompey, was partly political.

Scene 4

The scene shifts to Rome; but it is important to notice that although Antony isn't present, he remains the centre of interest. The audience knows – but Caesar doesn't – that Antony has decided to return, and that he is already on his journey. We are liable, therefore, to discount some of Caesar's complaints. It is apparent from the tone of his speeches, that the two men are temperamental opposites, their virtues, no less than their vices, diametrically opposed. The cautious and well-behaved Caesar inevitably regards Antony's behaviour as immoral, and, even worse, undignified. Then he is very conscious that he has been slighted. Whether by accident or design, Antony has treated him as an inferior, rather than as a partner. He is shocked by Antony's licentiousness, luxury and 'ef-feminacy', especially when contrasted with his former military toughness after his retreat from Modena, a few years before, when they had been fighting on opposite sides. Above all, Caesar needs Antony's prowess as a soldier because of the serious threat posed by Pompey and by piratical incursions. Neither Caesar nor Lepidus is in Antony's class as a soldier, so that, despite all the invective, it is plain that Antony's presence is desperately·needed. Lepidus is depicted, as he had been in *Julius Caesar*, as 'a slight, unmeritable man, / Meet to be sent on errands'. In this scene he tries to qualify Caesar's criticisms of Antony, and he is pathetically anxious to be kept informed of what is going on. His intervention at line 71 is ignored by Caesar, whose next line metrically completes his previous one.

Caesar's speech about the fickleness of the common people was a subject often touched on by Shakespeare, for example in *Coriolanus*, written soon after *Antony and Cleopatra*, and it was a favourite illustration of the dangers of democracy. But in Ulysses' speech on the power of time (in *Troilus and Cressida*) it is stated that everyone, not merely the common people, is subject to the same failing. The speech is nevertheless characteristic of Caesar and it contrasts with the attitude of Antony to those who desert from him.

Several editors (from Edward Capell to M. R. Ridley) introduce a second messenger at line 47 and they are surely right (although this does not appear in the Penguin edition). The news in the following lines, relating to the pirates, comes from a different source from that relating to Pompey; and 'Caesar, I bring thee word' is more natural in the mouth of a recently arrived messenger than as a continuation of the previous speech.

A word should be said about the style of the Messenger speeches. The second, in particular, seems somewhat inflated, and unnecessarily complex. Comparatively simple meanings are wrapped up in conceited language:

> Makes the sea serve them, which they ear and wound
> With keels of every kind . . .
> The borders maritime
> Lack blood to think on't, and flush youth revolt.

We have to work out that the people on the coasts are pale with fear, whereas the young, ruddy with health, join Pompey's forces. Shakespeare's messenger speeches in other plays are sometimes in a similar style (e.g. the messenger who warns Claudius of Laertes's rebellion; there the warning is blunted by the elaboration).

Scene 5

Back in Egypt, we are shown Cleopatra's reactions to Antony's absence, and the whole scene is devoted to this: Antony was the central topic in scene 4, as he is in this, in neither of which he is present. Cleopatra can now confess her love without the teasing and provocation she exhibits in his presence.

Antony's virility, and Cleopatra's response to it, is emphasized throughout the scene. Her taunting of the eunuch's sexual limitations and his fantasies about what Venus did with Mars lead directly to Cleopatra's musing about Antony. The horse that is happy to bear the weight of Antony is a way of saying that she would like to bear his weight. He is a demi-Atlas (i.e. a demi-demi-god) because he and Caesar bear the earth on their shouders. Lepidus, the third triumvir, can be left out of account. That Antony calls Cleopatra 'my serpent of old Nile' identifies her with Egypt, but there is also, of course, a sexual significance in his name for her. There is even a suggestion that Antony has succeeded the Sun as her lover: her sunburn or 'tawny front' is ascribed by her to 'Phoebus' amorous pinches'. The 'delicious poison' of which she speaks is the flattering idea that Antony is thinking of her, and loving her in spite of her wrinkles, and in spite of her amorous experience with Julius Caesar and the great Pompey. Shakespeare knew that this was not Pompey the Great, but his son; but he may have wished to give a temporary impression that Cleopatra had had love-affairs with the two greatest Romans of her time, and that she regarded Antony as their superior as a lover, and even as a man. Her description of herself as 'a morsel for a monarch' is an example of the frequent food imagery, reducing sex to a mere physical appetite, and reducing herself to a sex object. (See p. 56–7 for a discussion of this imagery.) This was in her salad days, when she was young and inexperienced, and so unable to make relevant comparisons. As Plutarch remarks, 'Caesar and Pompey knew her when she was but a young thing, and knew not then what the world meant'. The arrival of Alexas with Antony's gift and the promise that the pearl is only an earnest of the kingdoms he will give her – his implementation of this promise is the main cause of the war between Caesar and Antony –

seems to be the fulfilment of Cleopatra's day-dreams. Antony loves her in absence as much as in her presence. His marriage to Octavia is totally unexpected and a crushing disappointment.

Charmian's praise of Caesar is, of course, intended to tease her mistress. Some editors think that she is cowed by Cleopatra's threat to give her bloody teeth. I can see no evidence that she is cowed, and this is to misunderstand the relationship between Cleopatra and her maids. Their devotion to her is apparent by their willing suicide, which casts a retrospective light on their relationship early in the play.

The last two lines of the scene are printed as prose in the First Folio, but it contains a hidden couplet (*day* rhyming with *away*). The editorial rearrangement of the lines leads to the abandonment of the rhyme, and two short lines.

Act II

During this act – and we must remember that the division into acts was not that of the dramatist – the danger from Pompey and the pirates to the triumvirate brings about a temporary reconciliation between Antony and Caesar, cemented, as they hope, by the marriage arranged between Antony and Octavia, Caesar's half-sister (this was apparently Plutarch's error: she was Caesar's full sister). The failure of the marriage, foreseen by Enobarbus, proves to be an additional cause of friction between the two men. Shakespeare telescopes events and omits the period when the marriage seemed to be successful, with the birth of several children; and he brings forward Antony's decision to return to Egypt. Shakespeare was not writing a chronicle history and he altered the facts to suit his dramatic intentions. The historical Antony seemed to have left Cleopatra for good (see pp. 12 and 87).

Cleopatra is at first horrified to hear of the marriage, but in the continuation of the scene with the Messenger who has brought the news (II.5), separated by five scenes elsewhere, she recovers her confidence that Antony will return to her.

The succession and alteration of brief scenes, which early critics deplored, and which caused some of them to demote the play from tragic status, is a means of displaying the world scene on which the action was being played, and the world stakes which were involved. We move from Rome to Egypt, from Egypt to Misenum; and, in the following act, to Syria, Rome, Egypt, Athens and elsewhere. The places are not specifically mentioned in the dialogue: we deduce them from the characters who appear in the various scenes and from their intended movements. The function of the scene changes is discussed at length in Chapter 2.

Scene 1

We know from previous scenes that Antony has left Egypt, but Pompey still hopes that he will not leave Cleopatra. She had been Pompey's brother's mistress when she was still young, and there is something distasteful in his moralizing, and unpleasant in his sneers at her ageing – her 'waned lip'. Lust, love, witchcraft and *cordon bleu* cookery are combined, Pompey thinks and hopes, to make Antony oblivious of his honour – an 'honour' which consists in warring against Pompey. Shakespeare is preparing the way for Pompey's hypocrisy in Act III, but he has some reason, as we learn later, to bear a grudge against Antony.

When news arrives that Antony is expected in Rome, Pompey comforts himself with the thought that this should make them think more highly of themselves since the great Antony regards them as a serious threat, enough to detach him from Cleopatra; but he is shrewd enough to realize that, despite their differences and because of the common danger, Caesar and Antony may patch up their quarrel. What Pompey had called 'a petty war' (34) makes the hostility between the triumvirs seem a 'petty difference'. (49)

We learn from a later scene (II.6) that Pompey's ostensible cause is that of his father – defending the republic against dictatorship. But we also learn that his avowed war-aim is a screen for his naked pursuit of self-interest. The opening speeches of the present scene, considered in the light of later events, read like a public relations exercise. The appeal to the gods, modified by Menecrates' warning that the gods often deny us for our ultimate good, gives place to Pompey's reliance on his increasing popularity and power – if only Antony stays out of it. When it is apparent that Antony is about to arrive, Pompey again refers to the will of the gods.

Two textual points need comments:

1. line 39: *greet*: Ridley, following an earlier conjecture, argued that this was a misprint for *'gree'*.
2. The names *Menecrates* and *Menas* are liable to be confused in speech-prefixes (i.e. *Mene.* and *Men.*) and as Pompey addresses Menas at 42, all editors have emended the speech prefix to *Men.* at 38. Some editors, including Emrys Jones, have also emended two other prefixes at

16 and 18, following E. Malone's suggestion; and Samuel Johnson wanted to eliminate Menecrates altogether. But one gets the impression that Menecrates is an inferior and given to pious moralizing, and it is more appropriate for him to be snubbed (18, 19) than Menas.

Scene 2

With one exception – the last scene of all – this is the longest scene in the play, and one of the most important, for it seals Antony's fate. The opening dialogue between Lepidus and Enobarbus reveals once more Lepidus's fussy anxiety and his wish to be in with both sides, which results, in the end, in his being deserted by both. Enobarbus, here and later in the scene, exhibits his talent for plain speaking and his irritation with diplomatic evasions. It is also apparent that, notwithstanding his critical opinion of Cleopatra – indeed, of all women – and his view of Antony's enslavement, he is a staunch supporter of his general at this point in the play. As he is to a large extent a choric commentator, who mediates the author's point of view to the audience, we look at the conference through his sceptical eyes.

Antony's answers to Caesar's accusations are for the most part frank and honest. He shows that although he admired Fulvia's spirit, he was not responsible for her actions, and he hints that if Caesar had such a wife he would be equally unable to control her. He shows, too, that his brother was opposed to himself as well as to Caesar because he supported the republican cause. Caesar's most serious charge is that Antony had broken his oath to lend him arms and aid when required. Antony admits that the charge is serious as it impugns his honour. He blames the 'poisoned hours' which had prevented him from self-knowledge; he is forced to 'play the penitent' and offers the excuse that Fulvia's war was a ploy to separate him from Cleopatra. This was Plutarch's view. She 'raised this uproar in Italy, in hope thereby to withdraw him from Cleopatra'. Although Lepidus hurriedly interposes that Antony's partial apology ('So far ask pardon as befits mine honour / To stoop in such a case') is nobly spoken, it is difficult to avoid the conclusion that Antony had broken – or as he preferred to put it, 'neglected' – his oath.

Maecenas, aware of the urgent danger from Pompey, urges Caesar and Antony to forget their grievances; and Enobarbus tactlessly suggests that they can resume their wrangling when Pompey has been defeated. Caesar wishes he knew how to ensure their friendship: 'What hoop should hold us staunch'. This is Agrippa's cue for proposing the marriage of Antony and Octavia. It seems clear that Caesar knew of the proposal beforehand, and may even have suggested it himself. Although he professes to love his sister dearly – and there is no reason to doubt his sincerity in this matter – the arranged marriage is for political reasons, and the widow Octavia is a pawn in a political game. We do not know if Caesar was aware at this time that a breakdown of the marriage would give him a good excuse to defeat Antony and become the emperor of the whole Roman world.

As soon as the triumvirate have departed, the conversation naturally turns to the subject of Egypt. Enobarbus has a captive audience, for Maecenas and Agrippa want to hear the latest gossip, to know whether the rumours were true about the extravagant living in Alexandria and whether Cleopatra was as attractive as people said. Enobarbus describes Antony's first meeting with her on the river Cydnus, a description closely based on the most vivid passage in Plutarch's life of Antonius, superbly rendered by North (see p. 14). But Shakespeare's additional touches make it even more marvellous, and the picture of Cleopatra even more enchanting, as though he were remembering, but not mentioning, the rumour that it was a meeting of Venus and Bacchus 'for the general good of all Asia'. What makes it all the more remarkable is that the description is put into the mouth of the plain-speaking, unromantic soldier, and that he indulges in exaggerated conceits and hyperboles. She beggared all description; she o'erpictured pictures of Venus, and so on. Enobarbus's audience are suitably impressed – 'O, rare for Antony!' 'Rare Egyptian!' 'Royal wench!' As she captivated Caesar, Agrippa implies, it is no wonder that Antony was conquered too. But Enobarbus's enthusiastic description has a practical point: it is designed to show Maecenas and Agrippa that, in spite of the marriage to Octavia, Antony will not be able to leave Cleopatra:

> Age cannot wither her, nor custom stale
> Her infinite variety. Other women cloy
> The appetites they feed, but she makes hungry,
> Where most she satisfies; For vilest things
> Become themselves in her, that the holy priests
> Bless her when she is riggish.

Maecenas mentions the beauty and virtues of Octavia, but the audience is left with the impression that Enobarbus is likely to be proved right by events. Maecenas and Agrippa still hope that Antony will settle down with Octavia.

Scene 3

This short scene contains a sudden reversal. At the beginning it looks as though Antony intends to make his marriage work; at the end he decides to return to Egypt as soon as he gets an opportunity. He promises Octavia that he will turn over a new leaf ('all be done by th'rule') and suggests that rumour has exaggerated his blemishes.*

Plutarch leaves open the question of the Soothsayer's motives, whether it was 'to please Cleopatra, or else that he found it so by his art'. Shakespeare nowhere suggests that he was employed by Cleopatra to persuade Antony to return to Egypt (she did not yet know of his marriage). That the Soothsayer should regret that Antony ever went to Egypt in the first place, even though this might seem to conflict with his advice that he should return, is an indication that his advice was disinterested. In a play written just before *Antony and Cleopatra*, Macbeth says that his genius was rebuked by Banquo's, as Antony's was by Caesar. The genius, or guardian angel, of Antony, was afraid of Caesar's, 'and being courageous and high when he is alone, becometh fearful and timorous when he cometh near unto the other'. Antony confirms that Caesar always beats him when they play at dice or cock-fighting, and the fact that Caesar's fortunes are rising, while his are declining is an additional reason for returning to Egypt. It might not have weighed so heavily if he were not anxious to rejoin Cleopatra. Antony admits that the marriage was one of convenience, but his pleasure lies in the East. He does not immediately carry out this decision, but the interval before his return is much shorter in the play than it was in reality.

The instructions to Ventidius show that Antony is still concerned with that part of the Roman world belonging to his sphere of influence, and he wishes to gain glory by avenging the defeat of a Roman army by the Parthians and the murder of Crassus in 53 B.C. Julius Caesar's assassination took place when he was about to start on a Parthian campaign.

Scene 4

The main purpose of this tiny scene is to inform us that the triumvirs are to meet Pompey at Mount Misenum for a conference which may lead to war or peace. We also learn that Antony is outwardly on good terms with his bride.

* Line 8: *Good night, sir*. As Antony has already said good night to Caesar, and as Octavia has not replied to his 'Good night, dear lady', it is probable that the Second Folio was right in ascribing the second 'Good night, sir' to Octavia.

Scene 5

Cleopatra receives news of Antony's marriage, and the audience has been waiting for some time to see how she will react. Before the arrival of the messenger, she calls for music to minister to her love-melancholy, and Mardian is summoned to provide it. She changes her mind (showing how unsettled she is because of Antony's long absence) and asks Charmian to play billiards with her. As far as we know, billiards were not known in ancient Egypt, and Shakespeare has been ticked off for the anachronism. Then it was pointed out that in Chapman's play, *The Blind Beggar of Alexandria*, Princess Aspasia is told by her mother to 'send for some ladies to go play with you / At chess, at billiards'. From this Shakespeare could have learnt that billiards was known in Alexandria, and, moreover, how could a man with 'small Latin and less Greek' presume to question the authority of the learned translator of Homer? But Shakespeare often used anachronisms, not out of carelessness or ignorance, but rather to make the ancient world live again for audiences at the Globe.

Cleopatra refuses to play with Mardian because he is the antithesis of the masculinity she prizes, and now desperately misses, in Antony. The memories of their life together help to put the events of the play into perspective. The story of the dried fish attached to Antony's hook is recorded by Plutarch, although one unwary biographer ascribed the trick to the Dark Lady of the Sonnets. Another anecdote concerns a drunken, but harmless, frolic, when Cleopatra dressed Antony in her clothes, and she herself wore the sword he had used at the battle of Philippi, where Brutus and Cassius were defeated. It was doubtless a rumour of this transvestism which so shocked Caesar when he complained that Antony was

> not more manlike
> Than Cleopatra, nor the queen of Ptolemy
> More womanly than he;

The incident was intended by Shakespeare to remind us of Hercules, Antony's reputed ancestor, who exchanged clothes with his mistress, Omphale, on at least one occasion. Hercules' servitude to Omphale was often interpreted as 'an allegory of how easily a strong man becomes enslaved by a lecherous and ambitious woman'.

For the reception by Cleopatra of the news of Antony's marriage, Plutarch provided no information, and for the rest of the scene Shakespeare had to rely on his imaginative understanding of the character he had created. For the surprising physical violence used against the Messenger, Shakespeare took some hints from a much later episode, when Cleopatra is furious with Seleucus for not supporting her estimate of her treasure: 'Cleopatra was in such a rage with him, that she flew upon him, and took him by the hair of the head and boxed him well favouredly'. When he came to write the Seleucus scene, Shakespeare omitted the physical violence.

As a previous messenger had complained, 'The nature of bad news infects the teller', and Cleopatra is aware that she is being grossly unfair to the man who tells the truth. When she cools down, she confesses that her hands 'do lack nobility'. At the end of the scene, prostrated by Antony's infidelity, she wants a description of her rival and she admits that although Antony is a gorgon, looked at another way he is a Mars.

The scene continues, almost without a break, in Act III; but meanwhile we revert to what is happening in Italy.

Scene 6

The mention of hostages in the first line of this scene suggests that the conferring parties do not trust each other; and, indeed, in view of the massacre proposed by Menas in the next scene, they are wise to take precautions.

Pompey, like his father, had been opposed to Julius Caesar's concentration of power into his own hands, and is likewise opposed to the rule of triumvirate which equally reduces the powers of the senate. But since he agrees to the terms offered by Antony and Caesar without haggling, it looks as though purity of principle was less important to him than he had pretended. He has been bribed with Sardinia and Sicily; but in return he has to rid the sea of pirates – of which Menas is one – and supply Rome with wheat. It is not surprising that Menas asserts that Pompey the Great would never have signed such a treaty.

Pompey's remark about his father's house would only be understood by those members of the audience who had read Plutarch. Antony was living in Pompey the Great's house: he had bought it and then refused to pay, for reasons which are obscure. Shakespeare wanted to suggest that Pompey had a reason to be annoyed with Antony, but without going into details (which might have unnecessarily damaged our conception of him). Pompey in his cups is still harping on the matter (II.7.126). On another matter which makes Pompey harbour resentment – his hospitality to Antony's mother – Antony apologizes, as he had said earlier he would do (see II.2.155).

They agree to draw lots in the order of their four feasts, but it is not clear whether the banquet on Pompey's galley is the result of the ballot, or one of the projected feasts.

As soon as the leaders have left the stage, the other characters gossip about Egypt and about Cleopatra. As in the earlier scene (II.2) Enobarbus enjoys dispensing his inside knowledge. In Act II there are more than a dozen passages about Cleopatra and Egypt, and this is how Shakespeare ensures that the central theme of the play, Antony *and* Cleopatra, is never far from our thoughts. Enobarbus agrees with Menas that Antony's marriage is one of 'policy', not of love; and he prophecies that the marriage will prove to be 'the very strangler' of the amity of Antony and Caesar. Although he does not know of Antony's intention to return to Egypt, he knows that he will return to his Egyptian dish. The numerous references to Egyptian cooking and feasting reinforce the same idea.

Pompey refers to Cleopatra's love affair with Julius Caesar. Bernard Shaw, despite the birth of Caesarion, supposed that their relationship was purely platonic; but in *Caesar and Cleopatra* he dramatized the scene to which Pompey refers, in which Apollodorus conveys the queen to Caesar.

Scene 7

The world leaders are displayed in unbuttoned mood. Poor Lepidus, whose lack of importance is summed up by the servants, has already had too much to drink. He is so afraid of giving offence by declining a toast that he ends up drunk and incapable. Caesar, although he disapproves of wild parties, finds that his own speech is slurred. Antony and Enobarbus, accustomed to Alexandrian revels, are least affected and propose continuing their drinking at the end of the party.

Most of the conversation is again about Egypt. Antony gives Caesar a serious account of the importance of the Nile for the harvest, and then pulls the leg of Lepidus about the crocodile, who is too fuddled to realize he is being got at.

The song invoking Bacchus is clearly appropriate to the Bacchanalian revels; but we may also remember that Antony was associated not merely with Hercules, but also with Bacchus. As we have mentioned earlier, the first meeting of Cleopatra and Antony was rumoured to be a meeting of Venus and Bacchus; and the departure of Hercules in the play corresponds to the departure of Bacchus in Plutarch, who describes how they heard a marvellous sweet harmony of sundry sorts of instruments of music, with the cry of a multitude of people, as they had been dancing, and had sung as they use in Bacchus' feasts . . . it was the god unto whom Antonius bare singular devotion to counterfeit and resemble him, that did forsake them.

The main purpose of the scene, however, is the temptation of Pompey by Menas to assassinate the triumvirate. What is significant is not that he rejects the temptation – according to Plutarch he considers it for some time – but that he wishes Menas had carried out the murder without telling him. He wants the fruits of murder without having the responsibility for the actual deed. His claim that he puts honour before self-interest rings hollow. This is the unacceptable face of the power struggle in which the main characters are involved.

Act III

The central event of this act, precipitated by Antony's desertion of Octavia after bitter quarrels with Caesar, is the battle of Actium. Antony's soldiers begin to desert in ever increasing numbers what is plainly a losing cause. Caesar is irreconcilable because of Antony's treatment of Octavia; and, finding Cleopatra on amicable terms with Caesar's envoy, Antony suspects that she too is deserting him.

Scene 1

In this scene, concerned with the success of Ventidius's campaign against Parthia, we learn, with something of a shock, that Antony is jealous of his subordinates; but we should have been prepared for this by Antony's shame (I.2) at his own inactivity. Ventidius's remarks on the matter are of general application, and they refer to Caesar as well as to Antony. Such sentiments are not unknown in armies today.

> Who does i' th'wars more than his captain can
> Becomes his captain's captain; and ambition,
> The soldier's virtue, rather makes choice of loss
> Than gain which darkens him.

Although subordinates are often inclined to believe that they are better than their superiors, there is no reason to suspect that Ventidius is not speaking the truth. It should be added that Shakespeare omits altogether Antony's own disastrous Parthian campaign, as it was only marginally connected with his eventual fall.

Scene 2

In the first part of the scene two professional soldiers and cynical commentators give a satirical account of Lepidus's attitude towards the more powerful members of the triumvirate, and his difficulty in deciding which he most admires. This prepares the way for his sacking, reported in scene 5. Shakespeare suppresses some of the facts since they are not directly relevant to the quarrel between Caesar and Antony.

The remainder of the scene is devoted to the departure of Antony with Octavia. Despite his use of her for political purposes, it is apparent that Caesar is deeply attached to his sister; and Antony's two tender descriptions of her – 'The April's in her eyes' and

> Her tongue will not obey her heart, nor can
> Her heart inform her tongue – the swan's-down feather
> That stands upon the swell at the full of tide,
> And neither way inclines.

– make one wonder whether, after all, the marriage will be a success, despite Antony's previous resolution to return to Egypt. But it also appears that Octavia loves her brother more than her husband. Her feelings are delicately balanced, G. L. Kittredge observed, 'between sorrow at parting with her brother and desire to accompany her husband' that she is like a feather 'on the water when the tide is at the pause between flood and ebb'.

Caesar is afraid that Octavia, instead of being a cement to strengthen his friendship with Antony, may become the ram to batter its fortress; but Antony protests that his fears are groundless. We need not agree with those critics who imagine that Caesar had counted on Antony's providing him with a good excuse for war, and so enabling him to become the sole ruler of the Roman world. His anxiety is an indication of his love for Octavia, and a warning to the audience of what may happen.

The comments of Enobarbus and Agrippa on the tears of Caesar, comparing them to those of Antony after the deaths of Julius Caesar and Brutus, suggest that there is an element of insincerity in both the triumvirs.

Scene 3

This scene returns us to Egypt, and chronologically it follows immediately after I I.5 and precedes the intervening Roman scenes. We are led to assume that at approximately the same time as Cleopatra's interrogation of the messenger, all the non-Egyptian scenes have been taking place – the peace treaty between Pompey and the triumvirate, the banquet on board Pompey's galley, and the departure of the married couple from Rome. The splitting of the messenger scene has two dramatic advantages, besides the one mentioned earlier (p. 27): it bridges the gaps in space and time and helps to concentrate the attention on the relationship between Antony and Cleopatra and, by separating the gloom and fury of the first half from the renewed hope and confidence of the second, it prepares the way for Antony's return. This is made to seem more rapid than it would otherwise have done.

The interrogation of the messenger about Octavia is uncannily like Elizabeth I's questioning of Sir James Melville in 1564 about Mary, Queen of Scots. Sir John Neale describes the scene as reported by Melville in his memoirs:

Who, she asked, was the fairer, Mary or she? A question Melville tried to dodge by declaring that she was the fairest Queen in England, and theirs the fairest Queen in Scotland. As Elizabeth was not to be put off, he replied that they were both the fairest ladies of their courts, but the Queen of England was whiter. Next she wanted to know who was the higher. Mary was, answered Melville. Then is she over high, retorted Elizabeth; she herself being neither over high nor over low.

Questions followed about Mary's skill in playing and dancing, and Elizabeth later demonstrated her own skill in both respects.

Shakespeare was in his cradle at the time of this interview, and he is not likely to have heard of it, unless from one of James I's courtiers after the death of Elizabeth (Melville's memoirs were not published until long afterwards). But the incident shows the foolishness of a comment on Shakespeare's Cleopatra that 'she owes more to a study of prostitutes than to a knowledge of how even the worst queens behave'. Shakespeare knew that kings and queens were human and could be relied upon to act as such. He knew as well as Kipling that the Colonel's lady and Judy O'Grady were sisters under their skins.

The scene is richly comic in the contrast between Cleopatra's former rage against the Messenger for bringing ill tidings and her praise of his sensitivity and taste. He has learnt the hard way to be diplomatic. Charmian, who knows from experience what Cleopatra likes to hear, backs up the Messenger and supports the view that Antony will return: no doubt she is perfectly sincere in this conviction. At the end of the scene Cleopatra is about to write to Antony. She has good reason to believe that all will be well; and immediately Antony and Octavia enter for their last scene together, as though he had received Cleopatra's letter.

It will be noticed that Cleopatra hurriedly changes the subject when she hears that Octavia is thirty, as she herself is 'wrinkled deep in time'.

Scene 4

The peace between Antony and Caesar is already disintegrating, and the scene opens in the middle of a recital of Antony's grievances – including 'thousands more / Of semblable import' to those he has been rehearsing to Octavia. More seriously, Caesar has waged new wars against Pompey, without consulting Antony, and 'made his will, and read it / To public ear'. This is so curious an alteration of Plutarch's account that textual corruption has been suspected. Caesar had got hold of Antony's will from the Vestal Virgins, in whose keeping it was deposited, and read out extracts, including the clause that he wanted his corpse to be sent to Cleopatra, in order to smear his reputation. This incident took place a good deal later. Shakespeare, for reasons which are obscure, makes Caesar read out his own will, in which he made derogatory remarks about Antony. It could have been a simple lapse of memory, or Shakespeare may have felt that the audience would have been puzzled by the reference to the Vestal Virgins.

Caesar apparently damned Antony with faint praise:

> when perforce he could not
> But pay me terms of honour, cold and sickly
> He vented them . . .

Octavia urges Antony not to believe all the rumours; but Antony claims that his honour is at stake: 'If I lose mine honour, / I lose myself'. He agrees to Octavia going as a mediator, but says that in the meantime he will make preparations for war. He tells Octavia that she must ultimately choose between him and her brother. Dover Wilson declared that the lines

> our faults
> Can never be so equal that your love
> Can equally move with them

are Antony's 'own condemnation, and he knows it'. This is a peculiar interpretation of the words. Antony surely means that there are faults on

86

both sides, but he believes that he has greater cause for complaint, whatever Octavia thinks. One matter is left ambiguous: either Antony thinks that Octavia may bring about a reconciliation, or else he encourages her to visit her brother so that he can escape to Egypt.

Shakespeare avoids mentioning the lapse of time, and the fact that Octavia has borne one child to Antony and is pregnant with another when she leaves for Rome. He also suppresses the fact that Octavia did succeed in reconciling the two men. They came to an agreement at Tarentum, though immediately afterwards Antony returned to Egypt. Apart from the enticements of Cleopatra, Antony was ruler of the eastern half of the empire, so a visit to Egypt was necessarily on the cards.

Scene 5

This curious little scene packs so much information into twenty lines that no audience can be expected to follow it. Caesar used Lepidus in the war against Pompey and then imprisoned him, so that Caesar and Antony are now the sole contenders for supreme power. Pompey had been murdered by one of Antony's officers. Antony's navy is rigged 'for Italy and Caesar'. We are not told that it was thought that Antony, engaged in his Parthian campaign, had ordered the murder of Pompey who had fled to the island of Samos. Presumably Antony's navy is being prepared to fight Caesar's, though the actual battle was fought at Actium.

Scene 6

We now hear Caesar's side of the quarrel; but his complaints all relate to Antony's actions after his return to Egypt, which we hear about in the first words of the scene. Caesar begins in the middle of a string of complaints: Antony had criticized Rome; he and Cleopatra were enthroned in chairs of gold, with Cleopatra's children, including Caesarion, at their feet; Antony had confirmed Cleopatra as ruler of Egypt, and had given her other territories, and others to their sons; and Cleopatra had impersonated Isis. The territories given away were not Antony's but part of the Roman empire. The appearance of Cleopatra as Isis was regarded as blasphemy – if less blasphemous to us than the future deification of degenerate Roman emperors.

Antony, for his part, had complained that he hadn't been given his share of Sicily, that Caesar hadn't returned the ships he had borrowed, that Lepidus should not have been deposed without consultation, and that he ought to have shared in the spoil. These complaints and counter-complaints show that the entente is anything but cordial; but more serious, if unexpressed so far, is Antony's desertion of Octavia, which we may deduce from his presence in Egypt. The arrival of Octavia enables Caesar to unpack his heart. Characteristically he is more concerned with prestige, with the ostentation of his love, and with what people will say of him, than with Octavia's own feelings. Octavia is given a long list of the kings who have been enlisted as Antony's allies, a sonorous roll ingeniously adapted by Shakespeare from Plutarch, and doubtless fuelled by the Roman prejudice against kings since the expulsion of the Tarquins. The punishment of Antony for his treatment of Octavia now becomes a war aim, sanctified by the gods:

> the high gods,
> To do you justice, makes his ministers
> Of us and those that love you.

But it is clear from the beginning of this scene that there were more practical reasons for hostilities. The eastern half of the Roman empire was a threat to the west. Caesar regards the war as inevitable and urges Octavia to accept the fact without weeping. But the war was inevitable only because Caesar and Antony wanted incompatible things.

There is a neat contrast between the 'market maid', as which Caesar does not wish Octavia to appear, and Charmian's 'lass unparalleled' which is her epitaph on Cleopatra. Octavia is not the sort of person who wants an army for an usher, but Caesar believes that the existence of love has to be demonstrated by ostentation.*

Scenes 7–10

These four scenes are concerned with the battle of Actium, generally regarded as one of the decisive battles of the world. Shakespeare makes it plain that the result was due to Antony's foolish behaviour in deciding to fight at sea, and in following Cleopatra's flight. There was little actual fighting and Roman historians and poets exaggerated the part played by Caesar.

---

* Why Agrippa and Maecenas enter before Caesar at the beginning of the scene has not been plausibly explained. It may indicate that they have been discussing Antony's misdemeanours as Caesar enters.

Commentary

Scene 7

The opening dialogue between Cleopatra and Enobarbus is to emphasize her responsibility for the defeat. Enobarbus gives, under his breath, a bawdy objection to the presence of women in wars, and then a more polite explanation, that Cleopatra's presence is bound to prove a distraction.

Her question about 'denunciation' is variously interpreted. The Penguin editor, accepting Nicholas Rowe's emendation *Is't* (for *If*), points out that Caesar had declared war against Egypt, not against Antony. R. H. Case, retaining *If*, interprets: 'Even if the war were not proclaimed against me, what objection could you find for my presence?' Ridley, however, believes that 'denunciation' refers not to a declaration of war, but to a prohibition against her presence.

Shakespeare omits Antony's command to Cleopatra to return to Egypt, and the reason for her refusal – her fear that 'Antonius should again be made friends with Octavius Caesar, by the means of his wife, Octavia'. He also omits Cleopatra's bribery of Canidius to persuade Antony to adopt her policy. In the play Canidius does the opposite, arguing against fighting by sea, and deploring Cleopatra's influence: 'So our leader's led, / And we are women's men'.

Antony's professed reason for fighting by sea is the absurd one that Caesar had dared him, but no doubt he also does not wish to cross Cleopatra. He ignores the arguments of Enobarbus – that their sailors are conscripts, not the veterans of Caesar's fleet – and the heartfelt appeal of the anonymous and experienced soldier, not to trust to rotten planks. This appeal was based on Plutarch, whose soldier speaks of 'vile brittle ships' and refers to Phoenicians and Egyptians. Obviously Antony is behaving unwisely, but in view of the defeat of the Armada by English ships, and of Elizabeth I's courage in 1588, not all Shakespeare's original audience would have condemned Cleopatra.

Scenes 8, 9

These brief scenes suggest the preparations for the battle by the opposing leaders. Antony goes aboard during the countermarching mentioned in the stage direction at the beginning of the next scene. The battle itself is conveyed by noise alone.

Scene 10

Enobarbus has witnessed the flight of Cleopatra and her sixty ships, but not Antony's following of her. Scarus makes it clear that until Cleopatra fled, the two sides seemed evenly matched, with Antony's having a slight advantage – 'a pair of twins ... ours the elder'.*

Antony's behaviour, it is implied, is the first occasion when he has betrayed his manhood and military honour. Ruined by Cleopatra's evil magic, he is nevertheless a noble ruin. His conduct is the direct cause of a whole string of desertions. Canidius justifies his own by the precedent of the six royal allies of Antony who have already gone over to Caesar. Enobarbus remains loyal, although against his better judgement. Here Shakespeare departs from Plutarch, who records that Enobarbus deserts before the battle of Actium. Shakespeare wanted to make the battle as significant as possible, and he needed to retain his choric figure as long as possible.

Nothing is made by Shakespeare of the objections by Antony's troops to their fighting for Egypt against Rome. Officially, as we have seen, Caesar was not at war with Antony. Such a motive would have weakened the sense we have that the desertions were directly due to Antony's misjudgement, his declining fortunes, and his enslavement to Cleopatra.

Scene 11

The location for this scene is unspecified. It is generally assumed to take place in Egypt, although it makes use of Plutarch's vivid account of Antony sitting in the prow of Cleopatra's ship, and saying 'never a word, clapping his head between his hands – and so lived three days alone without speaking to any man'. Then Cleopatra's maids bring her to speak with Antony, so that they are reconciled. In the play Antony is equally ashamed and in despair. The course he has resolved on is either suicide or surrender to Caesar (9). He proposes to give away his treasure and urges his soldiers to make their peace with Caesar, promising to write on their behalf.

Shakespeare must have seen the significance of the name of the man who is called upon to kill Antony, and he uses Eros in this scene to bring the lovers together. This was his invention: Plutarch, as we have seen,

---

* No one knows the meaning of *ribaudred*, if that is what Shakespeare wrote, but from the association with leprosy, which was thought to be an appropriate disease for prostitutes, it presumably implies licentiousness.

tells how the reconciliation was brought about by Cleopatra's maids. Antony does not at first notice the approach of Cleopatra and the others. His remarks 'No . . . O, fie . . . Yes, my lord . . . I have offended' are not addressed to anyone present, but to an imaginary interlocutor. Antony blames himself, but he contrasts his own deserved reputation as a soldier with that of the man who has defeated him.

Neither Plutarch, nor Shakespeare himself in *Julius Caesar*, makes any mention of a hand-to-hand fight between Cassius and Antony, and Antony was only indirectly responsible for Brutus's death; but it is true that he was largely responsible for the defeat of the conspirators at Philippi, Caesar being indisposed at the time. Shakespeare here heightens the contrast between the warrior and his rival. He may have been reminded of Caesar's indisposition by the words of Garnier's *Antonie*:

> When Cassius and Brutus ill betide
> Marcht against us, by us twise put to flight,
> But by my sole conduct: for all the time
> Caesar hart-sick with feare and feaver lay.
> Who knowes it not?

Antony reproaches Cleopatra not so much for her cowardice – what she calls her 'fearful sails' – as for her not realizing that he was bound to follow her. But he soon forgives her, declaring that a single kiss repays him for his ruin. The lovers are reduced to sending Euphronius, the schoolmaster to their children, as ambassador to Caesar. Since the lovers have not been on speaking terms, it would appear that Antony alone was responsible for this move: this may be the resolution he refers to at the beginning of the scene: to ask Caesar's permission to live in Egypt or, failing that, as a private man in Athens. In the next scene, however, we learn that Euphronius comes as ambassador from Cleopatra as well.

Scene 12

The ambassador arrives in Caesar's camp, and Dolabella, who appears for the first time and is required for an important scene in Act V, points out that Antony is 'plucked'. Antony's requests show him, as he had foreseen (III.11.62) dodging and paltering in the shifts of lowness. He knows that his first request – that he should be permitted to live in Egypt – will be turned down; and the second request, to live privately in Athens, is not likely to be entertained by Caesar, who is bound to regard Antony as a permanent threat. Cleopatra realizes that she will be deposed and asks only that her heirs should inherit the throne. Caesar's object is to divide his two enemies, so he refuses Antony's requests and promises to give Cleopatra all she wants, provided that she drives Antony out of Egypt or murders him there. He then instructs Thidias to win Cleopatra from Antony by promising all she asks for, and anything else that occurs to him. Of course Caesar has no intention of honouring these promises. If his scheme works, he would be foolish to pay the bribe afterwards. He naturally has a low opinion of Cleopatra, because of her morals, but he thinks that women in general are an inferior sex:

> women are not
> In their best fortunes strong, but want will perjure
> The ne'er-touched vestal.

Scene 13

Enobarbus, interrogated by Cleopatra, does not blame her for being frightened by the battle, but condemns Antony for allowing his reason to be conquered by the itch of his affection, his passion, thereby nicking, or castrating, his position as commander.

Antony, entering with his returning ambassador, instructs him to inform Cleopatra of Caesar's terms. Her question 'That head, my lord?' shows, I believe, that she is not tempted to betray him to Caesar. Then Antony makes an absurd challenge to Caesar which will obviously be refused; for no one, least of all Caesar, would throw away his advantages and allow himself to be defeated in single combat. Enobarbus makes the acid comment:

> That he should dream,
> Knowing all measures, the full Caesar will
> Answer his emptiness! Caesar, thou hast subdued
> His judgement too.

In a continuation of his aside, Enobarbus recognizes that loyalty to fools is itself folly; but nevertheless,

> he that can endure
> To follow with allegiance a fallen lord
> Does conquer him that did his master conquer
> And earns a place i'th'story.

But, at the end of the scene, after witnessing more of Antony's strange behaviour, he comments that 'A diminution in our captain's brain / Restores his heart' and decides to desert.

Meanwhile he is present when Thidias arrives from Caesar, and naturally he misjudges the situation, thinking that Cleopatra is about to betray Antony. In fact her exclamation 'O!' to the suggestion that she had feared rather than loved Antony, is clearly ironical; so, too, is her agreement that her 'honour was not yielded, / But conquered merely', as the last word surely indicates. It is worth noting that Plutarch, when describing her last interview with Caesar when she is anxious to deceive him about her intentions, laid the blame for her action on her fear of Antony.

Following Caesar's instructions, Thidias asks Cleopatra what she requires of Caesar, since 'he partly begs / To be desired to give'. But there is a veiled threat that she must desert Antony:

> it would warm his spirits
> To hear from me you had left Antony . . .

Although 'shroud' means shelter, as intended by Thidias, it also has a more sinister meaning: both it and 'universal landlord' suggest that Caesar reigns over a kingdom of death.

Enobarbus arrives with Antony in time to see Cleopatra allowing Thidias to kiss her hand. It appears to Antony and Enobarbus, as well as to some critics, that she has been won over. Other critics believe that she is as likely to be deceiving Caesar here, as she does in Act V.

In his disgust at what he believes to be Cleopatra's treachery, her apparent willingness to send his grizzled head to Caesar, Antony looks back on his love affair, for which he has sacrificed at least half the world, and condemns his own love as merely vicious lust, as the poet of the Sonnets condemned his relationship with the Dark Lady, whether real or fictional, as 'the expense of spirit in a waste of shame'. He compares himself to a seeled falcon, temporarily blinded and stumbling about in the filth of the mews (see T. R. Henn's note, quoted in the Penguin edition). In the speech which follows Antony enumerates Cleopatra's most notorious liaisons, with Julius Caesar and Pompey's son, and others 'Unregistered in vulgar fame'. He uses food imagery to express his disgust ('morsel', 'fragment', 'picked out') as Troilus, after watching Cressida's surrender to Diomed, a few hours after she had vowed eternal fidelity, speaks of the scraps and greasy relics of her o'ereaten faith now given to his successor (see p. 57). Although Antony was a notorious womanizer, Shakespeare keeps quiet about this; and, in any case, with the different standards for men and women then prevailing, it would be natural for Antony to regard Cleopatra's conduct as immoral, while his own was perfectly normal.

It is, of course, Shakespeare's knowledge of the Psalms, rather than

Antony's visit to Palestine, which accounts for the mention of Basan (the spelling of the Psalter). The reference is to the horns which were supposed to adorn the brows of husbands whose wives had been unfaithful.

It was argued by Leslie Hotson that the terrene moon was the crescent-shaped formation adopted by the Spanish Armada in 1588 and referred to in Sonnet 107 in the line 'The mortal moon hath her eclipse endured'. The same formation, Hotson asserts, was adopted by the Egyptian fleet at Actium.[1] Antony's words would therefore mean simply that his fleet had been defeated, and that this defeat foreshadowed his own fall. But most critics believe that the mortal moon of the sonnet was Elizabeth I, and that the terrene moon was Cleopatra, the earthly embodiment of Isis. She is eclipsed, robbed of her divine attributes, by her negotiating with the enemy. As Antony, at this point in the scene, is still obsessed with Cleopatra's infidelity, this interpretation would seem to be more appropriate than a lament for his own defeat. A few lines later he declares that his severed navy has knit again.

Cleopatra's defence, which convinces Antony, is a reversal of the melting sweets image, the reversal, that is, of hypocritical flattery. If she were cold towards Antony, she wants the hail stones resulting from it to become projectiles to kill her, her offspring, and her 'brave Egyptians all'. Antony's mood completely changes, and he is now filled with courage and determination; but underneath is the realization that he is doomed. His proposal to have 'one other gaudy night' and to summon all his sad captains are signs that he knows that he has reached the end of the road. It is Shakespeare's way of dramatizing the confraternity described by Plutarch of those who will die together. But Antony's superficial and irrational optimism convinces Enobarbus that he is out of touch with reality, and reluctantly he decides to desert.*

---

* It is worth noting that there are two Shakespearian image-clusters in this scene (clusters of words which are triggered off without the knowledge of the poet). One of these has been mentioned (p. 60), that of flatterers, dogs and melting sweets, which is incompletely present. It starts with *melts* (90) and *feeders* (109), fades away, and resurfaces much later in *dissolve* (162) and *discandying* (165). The other cluster is set going by *kite* (89) – a bird which Shakespeare seems to have detested. It is Lear's word for Goneril. A mention of the word, as Edward A. Armstrong demonstrated in *Shakespeare's Imagination*, leads unconsciously to references in the same context to bed, death, spirits, and food. In the present scene we have *pillow* (106), *dying* (95), *devils* (89), and *feeders* (109).

Act IV

This act is concerned with the fall and death of Antony. After the battle of Actium, we realize that his days are numbered, and the sense of doom is brought home to us by a number of touches; by his foolishness in challenging Caesar to single combat, by the farewell feast envisaged in the second scene, by the desertion of Hercules in scene 3, by Enobarbus's desertion in scene 5, by Caesar's well-founded confidence that the war is in its final stages (scene 6), by the desertion of Cleopatra's fleet in scene 12, and in the taciturn gloom of the augurers. But the drift towards death is alleviated by occasional flashes of hope, when Antony achieves a temporary success in the 'royal occupation' (scenes 4–8).

Antony decides on suicide before he hears the false report of Cleopatra's death, a report which only hastens the inevitable; but the report means he can die for love, as well as to avoid disgrace. His death therefore parallels that of Cleopatra, whose suicide has equally mixed motives.

Scene 1

Caesar, incensed by Antony's calling him 'boy', retaliates by calling him 'the old ruffian'. (North misunderstood Amyot's French version of Plutarch, and Shakespeare followed North in the mistake. Caesar had said that Antony has many other ways to die; but Shakespeare's version, although erroneous, is dramatically much more effective.)

Caesar means to fight the last of many battles on the following day. As he says in scene 6, 'The time of universal peace is near'. It was thought by Church Fathers that the general peace in the Roman world, which preceded the nativity of Christ, was a sign from heaven. Milton described this in his 'Ode on the Morning of Christ's Nativity':

> No war or battle's sound
> Was heard the world around,
> The idle spear and shield were high up-hung:
> The hooked chariot stood
> Unstain'd with hostile blood,
> The trumpet spake not to the armed throng;
> And kings sate still with awful eye,
> As if they surely knew their sovran Lord was by.

The feast ordered by Caesar, supplied by the 'waste' the soldiers have earned, contrasts with the more personal, friendly and generous way

95

Antony treats his servants in the following scene. The juxtaposition was clearly deliberate.

Scene 2

This scene shows Antony in a most attractive light. He is entirely without condescension, and speaks to his servants as equals – there must be more than four, as Antony addresses six – putting them on a level with the kings who once served him. He declares touchingly that he is married to their good service, echoing perhaps the vow in the Anglican marriage service, 'for better, for worse, for richer, for poorer, in sickness and in health ... till death do us part'. Antony knows that he is doomed, although he pretends that he has been misunderstood. Murry speaks of the scene as Antony's Last Supper, although the actual supper, with the captains, takes place off stage, and though the servants have still to serve their master for one last time. There are, perhaps, analogies to the Betrayal of Christ, when Enobarbus dies of remorse, as Murry suggests in *Shakespeare* (1936).

Shakespeare did not dramatize the section of Plutarch's Life, in which Antony forsakes the company of his friends to lead Timon's life, because Antony too had suffered from men's ingratitude. Shakespeare had already used this passage in his play about Timon. Nor did he show Antony's return to Alexandria, which was followed by feasting and dancing, and the setting up of 'the order and agreement of those that will die together', whose members feasted each other in turn. But this may have coloured the mood and behaviour of Antony in several scenes in Act IV.

Plutarch mentions that Antony would 'drink like a good fellow with everybody, to sit with soldiers when they drink, and to eat and drink with them soldierlike – it is incredible what wonderful love it won him amongst them'. This breaking-down of the military class barrier was one of the things that outraged Caesar.

Scene 3

Antony's fate is foreshadowed in this mysterious scene – the only use of the supernatural in the play – in which Hercules leaves Antony. Here Shakespeare deviates from Plutarch, who speaks of Bacchus leaving Antony. Antony, as we have seen, was associated with Bacchus when he first encountered Cleopatra on the river Cydnus, and Bacchus is celebrated in the song on Pompey's galley. Shakespeare made the change because Antony prided himself on his resemblance to Hercules, his reputed ancestor, and because he wished to refer later to Hercules's dying rage (see IV.12.43). The god, as Emrys Jones points out in his commentary, symbolized Heroic Virtue. The matter is brilliantly discussed by Eugene M. Waith in *The Herculean Hero* (1962).

Scene 4

After the sense of an ending in scene 2 and the ominous signs in scene 3, Antony appears to have regained his confidence. He looks forward to the royal occupation of fighting. Cleopatra, after an initial attempt to detain him, shows herself as a good comrade, a soldier's wife; and Antony subdues his passion for her to his duty as a soldier. The business of arming is amusing and tender. Antony gives Cleopatra a hurried soldier's kiss. She is proud of her Herculean warrior, but she is enough of a realist to know that although Antony would be more than a match for Caesar in single combat, wars are not now settled in such a legendary and romantic fashion.

Scene 5

Antony now admits that he was wrong to fight at sea. Enobarbus has at last deserted and we are shown Antony's generous response to the news. Shakespeare adds two details to Plutarch's account. Antony does not merely forward Enobarbus's treasure; he sends 'gentle adieus and greetings', and, as we afterwards learn, he adds a gift of his own. He does not blame the deserter, but rather his own declining fortunes which have corrupted honest men. He does not add that his declining fortunes are themselves partly due to his own errors of judgement and his subservience to Cleopatra.

Scene 6

Shakespeare omits Plutarch's statement that Enobarbus was suffering from an ague when he deserted: it was against his dramatic purpose to have him die from natural causes. Nevertheless, as with so many events in the course of the play, his death has more than one cause. From the outset Enobarbus realizes that he has blundered. Caesar gives no honourable trust to deserters from Antony's army – one could hardly expect otherwise. Alexas, who actually persuaded Herod to change sides, is hanged for his pains. Caesar puts the deserters in the front line so that they have to fight their former comrades. Enobarbus says that he will 'joy no more'. It is at this point that he hears of Antony's generosity – that he is godlike, compared to Jupiter, in his bounty. The sense of shame, added to his realization that his desertion was a foolish mistake, is what 'blows' Enobarbus' heart. He expects to die of the shock, but he seems to imply that otherwise he will commit suicide.

Scene 7

At the end of this scene Antony exits and reappears at once at the beginning of scene 8. This violates a well-established convention that a character should not re-enter immediately, but this might be excused by the 'alarum' which could be thought to separate the two scenes. Another convention is that when the stage is cleared (as at the end of line 3) a new scene should be marked. The first of these conventions could be restored if Agrippa's lines (1–3) were transferred to the end of the scene, and his order to retire would be appropriately followed by Antony's words at the beginning of scene 8.

Scene 8

Agrippa, Caesar's general, has been forced to retreat, and Antony celebrates what proves to be his last victory. The chivalric term *gests* (an emendation for *guests*, which doesn't make sense) shows that he dedicates his and his soldiers' triumph to his queen, his enchantress, 'this great fairy'. She greets him with the splendid question:

> Lords of Lords!
> O infinite virtue, com'st thou smiling from
> The world's great snare uncaught?

The world's great snare is not merely the uncertainty of war, but the worldly principles opposed to their love, ultimately Rome and all it stands for. Antony responds to the lyrical perfection of Cleopatra's greeting with the words 'My nightingale'. Cleopatra promises Scarus an armour of gold. It is interesting to note that Shakespeare suppresses the sequel to this scene, as related by Plutarch: 'howbeit the man at arms when he had received this rich gift, stole away by night and went to Caesar'. Mention of this desertion might have spoilt the Enobarbus scene which follows. Scarus is still loyal to Antony in scene 12.

Scene 9

Enobarbus, searching for a ditch in which to die, wishes to be remembered as a traitor, but one who has repented; and he wants to be
forgiven by Antony – a forgiveness already freely granted – but not by
others. He compares himself to a runaway slave, a master-leaver, one at
the very bottom of the social pile (Murry comments that this is the story
of Judas, 'told as it might have been had a Shakespeare been there to tell
it').

Enobarbus' last two speeches are highly wrought, with an unusual
amount of subtle alliteration:

> O sovereign *m*istress of true *m*elancholy,
> The *p*oisonous *d*amp of night *d*isponge u*p*on *m*e,
> That *l*ife, a very re*b*el to my wi*ll*,
> May *h*ang no longer on me. Throw my *h*eart
> Against the *f*lint and *h*ardness of my *f*ault,
> Which, *b*eing dried with grie*f*, will *b*reak to *p*owder,
> And *f*inish all *f*oul thoughts.

Scenes 10–12

The surrender of the fleet to Caesar, the last of desertions from Antony
rather than a betrayal engineered by Cleopatra, means the final ruin of
Antony. It is prepared for by the fear of the augurers to interpret the
building of the swallow's nest in the sails of Cleopatra's ships, and by
Antony's alternating hopes and fears, as described by Scarus. When the
fleet fraternizes with the enemy, Antony immediately assumes that
Cleopatra is responsible; that she has come to terms with Caesar and
that Thidias's mission has succeeded. Despite his love, Antony never
wholly trusts Cleopatra; her play-acting and her infinite variety inevitably make her an object of suspicion, especially as Antony knew that he
himself was triple-turned – from Fulvia to Cleopatra, from Cleopatra to
Octavia, and from Octavia back to Cleopatra. He decides to commit
suicide, as the line 'O sun, thy uprise I shall see no more' and his
summoning of Eros (30) indicates. First he proposes to revenge himself
on Cleopatra; but when she appears, he does not carry out his threats,
warning her instead of the fate worse than death awaiting her as a
spectacle in Caesar's triumph, and as Octavia's victim. After Cleopatra
rushes out, terrified of his rage, Antony decides that her death will lead
to the immediate end of the war: 'one death might have prevented many'.
He therefore calls on Alcides (i.e. Hercules) to inspire him with rage

against Cleopatra. The poisoned shirt of Nessus was sent to Hercules by his wife, believing that its magical properties would ensure his fidelity to her. The story was well known to Shakespeare from Ovid's *Metamorphoses* and Seneca's play, *Hercules Oeteus*. Lichas, who innocently brought the shirt, is not lodged on the horns of the moon, but thrown into the sea,

> Whirled through the air three times, four times, flung far
> Toward the Euboean waters, as a stone
> Flies from a catapult.[2]

So Antony decides at the end of the scene to kill Cleopatra, 'The witch shall die'; but from the conversation with Eros in scene 14, he seems to be intent only on suicide.*

Scene 13

This scene follows Cleopatra's exit in the previous scene and is presumed to take place during Antony's soliloquy. The story of Ajax's madness is told by Ovid in the *Metamorphoses* (XIII) and the story of the boar of Thessaly in Book VIII. It is Charmian who suggests the false story of Cleopatra's death, and this minimizes the guilt of the Queen, especially as she later sends word to avert the suicide she fears.

Scene 14

Antony has thrice called for Eros, and at the beginning of this scene Eros has just answered the call, thus ensuring an impression of continuity. Hamlet had played on the shifting shapes of clouds as a means of baffling Polonius (III.2.381). Antony uses the same idea to show that he has lost his sense of identity, that he has been reduced to a shadow of his former self by Cleopatra's betrayal. Editors have quoted parallels to this speech from Pliny, Chapman, Du Bartas, Whetstone, and others. But althought Du Bartas mentions dragon, castles, rocks and mountains, Chapman mentions dragons and lions, and Whetstone lions, bears, pageant and monsters being conquered by Hercules, there is no need to find a particular source for what is a common experience.

It should be mentioned that Shakespeare, as often in his later plays,

---

* Antony's complaint that his followers have deserted him, less generous than his remarks on Enobarbus, is expressed in a famous image-cluster, mentioned above (p. 94). The mention of dogs leads to melting sweets and flatterers. This cluster supports the emendation *spanieled* (for *pannelled*).

uses irregular internal rhymes: bear/air; rock/mock; black/rack. The metaphor of Caesar and Cleopatra cheating Antony at cards, as Jones points out, ends with a quibble on *triumph*, another form of trump.

When Antony is told that Cleopatra is dead, he immediately decides to follow her:

> The long day's task is done,
> And we must sleep.

These lines are inadvertently echoed by Iras in the last scene of the play:

> the bright day is done,
> And we are for the dark.

The seven-fold shield of Ajax was made of brass, backed with seven layers of oxhide, so thick that Hector's dart could not penetrate it. Ovid in *Metamorphoses* (XIII) speaks of Ajax as the owner of the sevenfold shield, and Shakespeare could have read of it there or in Chapman's translation of *The Iliad*, part of which he had used in *Troilus and Cressida*.

This speech (37–54) is again highly wrought. It uses internal rhymes and half rhymes, while remaining blank verse: Apace/case; torture/torch; stray/yea/Stay; flowers/ours; want/haunt. 'Sprightly' is a quibble, meaning both high-spirited and ghostly.

Shakespeare has been pedantically condemned for ignorance in reconciling Dido and Aeneas in the underworld. He knew perfectly well that when Aeneas visits the underworld in Book 6, Dido companions her husband Sichaeus in Hades and turns away from Aeneas in disdain. Ridley comments that Shakespeare was not likely 'to uncouple a famous pair of lovers for a pedantic scruple'. This, I think, misses the point. For Shakespeare would also know that Virgil had not yet written his epic at the time Antony was speaking; he would know that it was fiction rather than history; and he was perfectly entitled to credit Antony with an alternative fiction, appropriate to his state of mind at the time.

The immediate occasion for Antony's suicide is the supposed death of Cleopatra: he feels ashamed that his mind is less noble than hers, that it lacks the courage of a woman. But he had already decided to kill himself rather than suffer the disgrace of being a part of Caesar's triumph. In the same way Cleopatra's suicide was primarily for love of Antony, but it was also to avoid the shame of being taken to Rome in Caesar's triumph.

The reminder to Eros of his promise to kill his master if the necessity should arise is similar to Cassius's request to Pindarus in the last act of

Julius Caesar and to Brutus's pleas to several of his followers to kill him. Pindarus does kill Cassius, and Strabo is finally persuaded to hold Brutus's sword on which to impale himself. That Eros killed himself rather than his master is another sign of the affection Antony inspires. The genuine grief of his soldiers and his complete absence of reproach on learning that Cleopatra had not really killed herself also add to his stature. So too, perhaps, do the echoes from the Apocalypse, which Ethel Seaton pointed out, beginning with 'The star is fallen'.[3] Yet some critics point to the bungled suicide and the refusal of the guard to put Antony out of his misery as a deliberate contrast to his noble speeches, and they stress the sordid reality of his end. But, of course, even without the vivid account given by Plutarch, which Shakespeare followed as closely as possible, it was only by an ineffective suicide that Antony could have the last, and most moving, meeting with Cleopatra.

Shakespeare, however, did not shut his eyes to realities. Nor did his characters. It is natural for Decretas to use Antony's sword as a means of ingratiating himself with Caesar: once Antony is as good as dead, his realistic followers, whatever their grief, look out for themselves.

Scene 15

There are two preliminary problems about this scene, one concerning staging, the other textual.

The traditional view of the staging is that Antony is hoisted to the balcony by Cleopatra and her maids. But J. Dover Wilson suggested in his edition that 'a flat-roofed wooden structure was brought on to the stage' and that Cleopatra and her maids would 'take their places on the roof'. A third view is that Antony was brought in at ground level, where the groundlings were standing, and was pulled up to the main stage.

The first method seems improbable. If Antony's death scene were staged on the balcony, he could not be seen by many members of the audience. Indeed, he would be invisible to all if his reclining body were behind the balustrade. Burbage would not have consented to playing the death scene in such conditions. Dover Wilson's method also seems to be very unlikely. The large monument, substantial enough to have at least four persons on the roof, and probably several others, would have to be brought on at the beginning of this scene, taken away at the end, and brought on again at the beginning of V.2. If it were left during V.1, Caesar could ignore its presence, though with some difficulty; but the long final scene had to be played on the full stage, partly because of the large number of characters present at the end – three dead women, the guard, Dolabella, Caesar and his train – and partly because such an important scene needed plenty of space for it to be dramatically effective. There seems to be little doubt that both IV.15 and V.2 were enacted on the main stage. A modern director will make his own arrangements, unaffected directly by the staging in Shakespeare's theatre.

Professor Joan Rees, in an article in *Shakespeare Survey* 6, suggested that Samuel Daniel had seen a performance of *Antony and Cleopatra*, and that the 1607 revision of his own play included a reminiscence of the hauling up of Antony:

> She drawes him up in rowles of taffaty
> T'a window at the top, which did allow
> A little light unto her monument.
> There Charmion, and poore Eras, two weake maids
> Foretir'd with watching, and their mistresse care,
> Tug'd at the pulley, having n'other aydes,
> And up they hoise the swounding body there
> Of pale *Antonius*, showring out his blood
> On th'under lookers, which there gazing stood.
> And when they had now wrought him up halfe way
> (Their feeble powers unable more to doe)
> The frame stood still, the body at a stay,
> When *Cleopatra* all her strength thereto
> Puts, with what vigor love and care could use,
> So that it mooves againe, and then againe
> It comes to stay when she afresh renewes
> Her hold, and with reinforced power doth straine,
> And all the weight of her weake bodie laies
> Whose surcharg'd heart more than her body wayes.

With the last of these lines Ridley compared Cleopatra's similar conceit (IV.15.33): 'Our strength is all gone into heaviness, / That makes the weight'.

The textual problem is more serious. If we assume that the text was printed from Shakespeare's manuscript – not from the prompt book – there may well be passages which would have been cut or emended in performance. Dover Wilson argued that lines 13–31 were a false start which should have been deleted by Shakespeare. Perhaps they were, and the deletion marks were overlooked by the editors or printers of the First Folio. The evidence that something has gone wrong is partly in some confusion about drawing up Antony. (Help, friends below! Let's draw him hither'; 'Help me, my women – we must draw thee up') and some repetition of ideas:

> Not Caesar's valour hath o'erthrown Antony,
> But Antony's hath triumphed on itself . . .
> .a Roman by a Roman
> Valiantly vanquished.

There is even a repetition of actual words: 'I am dying, Egypt, dying'. Some critics, including Jones, defend the Folio text, on the ground that the confused and repetitive nature of the scene illustrates Shakespeare's wish in this play to exemplify life's tendency to untidiness and anticlimax – to avoid what Stendhal called the great falsehood of art. But one cannot help feeling that such a method of deliberate untidiness would be a mistake: directors would be driven to clarify the action. In any case the repetition of 'I am dying, Egypt, dying' is unfortunate: it ruins the first use. So a tidying up of this scene is probably necessary. Yet it would be a great pity to lose Cleopatra's fear of being captured and her characteristic remark about Octavia 'demuring upon' her. We have to remember that some fifteen years had elapsed between performances and publication of the play and that changes were inevitably made between the time the poet delivered his manuscript and the end of rehearsals.

Cleopatra is convinced that Antony has killed himself before Diomedes arrives with the news, and she realizes that her terrified lie was the cause. She invokes the sun to burn the sphere in which it moves. The sun, as B. Heath explained, was thought to be a planet, and 'was whirled round the earth by the motion of a solid sphere in which it was fixed. If the sun therefore was to set fire to the sphere, so as to consume it, the consequence must be, that itself, for want of support, would drop through, and wander in endless space; and in this case the earth would be involved in endless night'.[4] Cleopatra wishes universal darkness to cover all, in mourning for the death of Antony.

She is so terrified of being captured that she dare not come down to receive Antony's last kiss. Her exclamation 'Here's sport indeed!' is not frivolous, as some have supposed, but a revelation of the strain under which she is suffering. She quibbles, as we have seen, on the two meanings of heaviness, weight and grief. Elizabethans did not regard puns as necessarily funny or a low form of wit, suitable only for clowns; and although Dr Johnson spoke of quibbling as Shakespeare's fatal Cleopatra for which he lost the world, quibbles have come back into favour in the present century as a serious poetic device.

Johnson also complained of the line 'That the false housewife Fortune break her wheel', calling it despicable and other critics have echoed his complaint. They don't object to Hamlet calling fortune a strumpet, but regard 'false housewife' as low. But the line fits in with Cleopatra's frequent attacks on fortune and on those fortune favours. The lowness is appropriate in its context. Eighteenth-century tragedies are so feeble, partly because their talented authors dared not be low.

Cleopatra is more clear-sighted than Antony both in her realization that honour and safety do not go together for her, and in her distrust of Proculeius who deceives her about Caesar's intentions and arranges her surprise and capture.

Antony's eulogy of himself was not intended by Shakespeare to be an expression of egotism or self-delusion, as some critics have supposed – as T. S. Eliot and F. R. Leavis believed perversely that Othello in his final speech was not making an objective defence of his actions, but merely cheering himself up. Antony 'is literally at his last gasp and his utterance is broken by heavy pauses' (Ridley).[5] This is suggested by the four full stops and two colons in the Folio text.

Cleopatra feels that the world, without Antony, is no better than a sty. The same idea is repeated in her dying words, completed aptly by Charmian; and it echoes Antony's proclamation that the dungy earth is redeemed from vileness only by their mutual love. In her lament ('O, withered is the garland . . .') Cleopatra recreates Antony as a super-human, almost a divine, figure, so that when the moon looks down, after his death, on the earth robbed of his presence, she sees that there is nothing wonderful remaining. The speech is an expression of abandoned grief, and it fuses many disparate ideas: of Antony as emperor, soldier and lover; as the pole star by which others guided their lives. Underneath there is a half-hidden image of the maypole with its phallic associations, and with boys and girls dancing around it.

When Cleopatra recovers from her swoon, she repudiates the royal titles with which she has been addressed by Iras, and claims that she is subject to the same passions as those at the bottom of the social scale. Perhaps because she remembers Cleopatra's words, Charmian in her speech of farewell calls her 'lass'.

Cleopatra's comparison of herself to a milkmaid – a Tess of the D'Urbervilles, one might say – has led to some strange reactions. It has been deplored as undignified, as a proof that she 'is governed by no specifically noble passion', as unqueenly. Real queens, however, talk in a variety of ways, some like Anne Boleyn, some like Queen Victoria, and others like the Red Queen in *Alice in Wonderland*. By a curious coincidence, Elizabeth I, when pressed by the Commons to take a husband, contrasted her position in 1576 with that of the maid who milks: 'If I were a milk-maid, with a pail on my arm, whereby my private person be a little set by, I would not forsake that poor and single state to match with the greatest monarch'.

Cleopatra's repudiation of her royal position, her wish to throw her sceptre at the injurious gods, is a gesture of revolt at the meaninglessness of life, the emptiness of the world since Antony is no longer in it to give it a meaning. She unconsciously echoes Antony's words, 'The torch is out' in 'Our lamp is spent, it's out'. Cleopatra was his light, as Antony was hers. Charmian and Iras become ennobled – they are called 'my noble girls' – comrades rather than servants, who willingly consent to a brave and noble suicide. Cleopatra, once the very antithesis of the spirit of Rome, decides to act 'after the high Roman fashion', converted by Antony's example and by his spirit.

Act V

This is Cleopatra's act. *Antony and Cleopatra* is the only one of Shakespeare's tragedies in which the heroine is given solitary importance in her death. The deaths of Cordelia and Desdemona are subordinated to those of Lear and Othello, and they die before the heroes; and although Juliet does live for a few minutes after Romeo, he is given a much longer and more impressive death speech.

At the end of the previous scene Cleopatra had decided to commit suicide along with her maids, her love of Antony intensified by his death for love of her. This motive is supported, and not contradicted, by her fears of Caesar's intentions. Egypt has been defeated and Rome is not normally generous to vanquished enemies. In spite of Julius Caesar's reputation for clemency, Vercingetorix languished in prison after the conquest of Gaul. There are moments during the rest of the play when the audience may suspect that Cleopatra's determination is weakening, that she may decide after all to go on living, provided she can avoid the shame of appearing in Caesar's triumph. But Caesar soon makes it clear to his intimates that he is determined on humiliating Cleopatra, although he tries to conceal his purposes from her. Several things, however, convince us that she really means to die: her experiments with poisons, her attempt to stab herself when she is captured, and the scene in which she attacks her treasurer.

Scene 1

Decretas arrives with Antony's sword, and we are given the reactions of Caesar and his associates to his death. They recognize the historical inevitability of the tragedy. Caesar knows he is responsible, but he himself would have been the victim of their quarrel if Antony had won, because they 'could not stall together in the whole world'. Caesar's followers can afford to praise Antony when he no longer represents a threat. Agrippa declares, 'A rarer spirit never / Did steer humanity'; and Maecenas observes that Caesar must see himself in the mirror provided by Antony's death. As indeed he does. He speaks of him as 'brother' – that is, primarily, but not entirely, as Octavia's husband – as

> my mate in empire,
> Friend and companion in the front of war,
> The arm of mine own body, and the heart
> Where mine his thoughts did kindle . . .

Caesar admits that the news of Antony's death is 'a tidings / To wash the eyes of kings'. Agrippa sees that Caesar is touched, and this is apparent not merely from his words, but also from his lapse of memory: he asks for Dolabella (70), not remembering that he had sent him to Antony at the beginning of the scene. Characteristically, he is anxious (as we noticed on his first appearance) to convince others of the rightness of his actions:

> Go with me to my tent, where you shall see
> How hardly I was drawn into this war,
> How calm and gentle I proceeded still
> In all my writings.

Meanwhile his chief concern is to prevent Cleopatra's suicide by sending Proculeius and Gallus to assure her that she will be honourably treated. Proculeius knows that this is a lie, but he obeys unhesitatingly.

One curious remark of Caesar's – 'For Caesar cannot *live* / To be ungentle' – is based on Nicholas Rowe's emendation of the Folio reading, *leave*. It may be suspected that the Folio is correct, but that some words were omitted by accident, or just understood. Caesar means to say that he cannot leave his normal humane behaviour and become cruel; but, by a slip, he says the opposite of what he intended.

Scene 2

As we have seen (p. 102), critics disagree about the staging of this scene, but I believe it is impossible that the monument should be represented by the balcony, and still more by the inner stage. Cleopatra's great ritual death needs the whole stage to be fully effective. As soon as she appears, the scene automatically changes from Caesar's camp to the monument, and it so remains for the rest of the play.

Mardian is given an entry at the beginning of the scene, but thereafter he is forgotten. He does not speak, and he is given no exit. His presence at the suicide would not be appropriate. Kittredge and others retained Mardian because he had to come to the monument to inform Cleopatra of Antony's reactions to her reported death. This is absurdly literal. Shakespeare doubtless found he was in the way and forgot to delete his entrance. It is another indication that the play was printed from Shakespeare's manuscript. Those who assume that Proculeius converses with Cleopatra through the gates seem to be unduly influenced by Plutarch's account, which Shakespeare was not bound to follow in every detail. It is probably best for Proculeius to enter alone, allowed in by the guards, as Cleopatra is anxious to find out Caesar's intentions.

Cleopatra's first speech is virtually a soliloquy, despite the presence of Charmian and Iras. It is a continuation of her thoughts on suicide begun immediately after Antony's death. There, the motive was that his death had deprived her life of meaning. Now it is a stoical scorn of the changes and chances of fortune. Like Horatio, who wanted to kill himself after the death of Hamlet, because he was 'more an antique Roman than a Dane', Cleopatra determines that she will not be fortune's slave, but rather be one who, in Hamlet's words, 'is not a pipe for Fortune's finger, / To sound what stop she please'. Cleopatra, in one sense, can be regarded as more Roman than Caesar himself who, she thinks, is fortune's knave and on a level with a common beggar, since they both depend for subsistence on the dungy earth. Cleopatra, who had mocked Antony when, in the first scene of the play, he had contrasted the nobleness of their love with the life of beasts and of men who feed on the dungy earth, is now echoing him. (The echo is enough to cast doubt on Theobald's emendation of *dug*, for *dung*, plausible though it might seem. It was probably written dũg.)

The entrance of Proculeius raises the question of whether he was privy to the plot to capture Cleopatra. Antony had recommended her to trust only Proculeius (IV.15.48), and it has been argued that this exemplifies his poor judgement, or even that he wanted to avenge himself on Cleopatra. Caesar's instructions to Proculeius in the previous scene, and his later words to Gallus, do not support the view that Proculeius was aware of the plot, though they do not disprove it. He knew he had the job of deceiving Cleopatra about Caesar's intentions. He was probably not aware that Gallus had other instructions.

Cleopatra realizes that as a defeated and hated enemy she can hardly expect freedom or mercy, but she has a faint hope that her son might be allowed to reign in her place. The way in which her request is couched, referring to herself as the vassal of Caesar's fortune, recalls her statement that he is fortune's knave. She thinks of herself, doubtless with irony, as a knave's vassal.

How Gallus and the soldiers gain entrance to the monument is of no great importance; and in any case the method used in the seventeenth century differed from that which might be used today. All that is important is that Cleopatra should be surprised (e.g. by a scaling ladder, or by treachery), as she would not be if the soldiers broke down the gate or door. Cleopatra is disarmed without difficulty, but this does not mean that her attempt to stab herself was a piece of play-acting. She wishes to die; and the reasons she gives are her unwillingness to face the disapproval of the virtuous Octavia, and the shame of appearing in Caesar's triumph and of being jeered at by 'the shouting varletry'. Although she treats Charmian and Iras as comrades, she has as much horror of the stinking plebians as Coriolanus had. Her preference for a ditch in Egypt, the mud of Nile, or to be hung in chains from a pyramid are an admirable use of local colour. Her threats to destroy herself and the message she sends to Caesar – 'Say I would die' – are ill advised, as it may lead him to take extra precautions.

Dolabella is Cleopatra's last, if inadvertent, conquest. He is described by Plutarch as 'one of Caesar's very great familiars, and besides did bear no evil will unto Cleopatra'. It is he who warns her of Caesar's intentions: 'He sent her word secretly, as she had requested of him'. Shakespeare took note of this and substituted Dolabella for one of Caesar's slaves, named Epaphroditus, at this point in the play. He appears to have taken hints from Daniel's *Cleopatra* in his treatment of Dolabella's love and pity for the heroine (see p. 20).

In Cleopatra's dream of Antony she depicts him not as he was, nor as she imagined him in his lifetime, but idealized, as a mythological figure. Some of the details of this speech, as Walter Whiter showed, were suggested by masques and pageants, which Shakespeare had seen or heard described:

Let it be remembered that an imitation of the sphere of the Heavens, with the attributes and ornaments belonging to it, the sweetness of the music, and the noise of its thunder, the Sun, the Moon, and the Earth, colossal figures – armorial bearings – a magnificent procession of monarchs and their attendants – floating islands – and a prodigal distribution of wealth and honours, are the known and familiar materials which formed the motley compound of the Masque, the Pageant, or the Procession.[6]

The effect of Cleopatra's description is to eliminate for the time Antony's blemishes, and to turn him into a demi-god. By increasing his stature she elevates her own. (It should be mentioned that nearly all editors have accepted Theobald's emendation, *autumn 'twas* for *Antony it was*, and this is doubtless the intended meaning. Nevertheless the change is unnecessary, for Cleopatra equates Antony and autumn, a quintessential, inexhaustible, bountiful autumn.) Antony's delights were dolphin-like, a word which implies playfulness, gaiety, and friendliness: his pleasures did not detract from his greatness. It is worth noting that in Virgil's account of the battle of Actium – it is represented on the shield presented to Aeneas by Venus, along with other scenes from Roman history – dolphins accompany Caesar's fleet, and their presence is a good omen:

> It was done in gold, yet it looked like the blue sea foaming with white-caps:
> Dolphins, picked out in silver, were cart-wheeling all around,
> Lashing the face of the deep with their tails, and cleaving the water.[7]

It is possible that Shakespeare remembered these lines and transferred the dolphins from Caesar to Antony. Plutarch, in his *Moralia*, said that

> the dolphin alone of all other creatures in the world by a certain instinct of nature, carrieth that sincere affection unto man, which is so much sought for and desired by our best philosophers without any respect at all of commodity: for having no need at all of man's help, yet is he nevertheless friendly and courteous unto all.

Shakespeare may have felt, after reading this tribute, that the dolphin was more appropriately connected with Antony than with the Caesar he had depicted; he may also have felt that Plutarch was nearer to the facts of history with regard to Actium than Virgil, who was anxious to make the most of Caesar's victory by exaggerating the strength of the opposition.

After hearing Cleopatra's eulogy of Antony, Dolabella implies, as gently as possible, that she is deluded; and she retorts that the real Antony was superior to her fantasy of him. As Dolabella sympathizes with her grief and with the expression of her love, he has no hesitation in revealing Caesar's intentions, and so thwarting them.

The arrival of Caesar leads to a nice exercise in mutual deception, Caesar pretending that he is going to be magnanimous, and Cleopatra pretending to believe him. Caesar's image of generosity is somewhat tarnished by his pretence of not being able to distinguish the queen from her maids, and still more by his threat to kill Cleopatra's children if she takes her own life. She tries to convince Caesar that she wishes to live;

and this is why she underestimates her treasure. Whether she had a prior arrangement with Seleucus is immaterial: perhaps his part in the interlude would be more effective if he were unaware of the queen's tactics. Plutarch makes it clear, and North makes it even clearer by a marginal note, that Caesar had been tricked. As we have seen, the physical violence used by Cleopatra, as described by Plutarch, was transferred by Shakespeare to the earlier scene in which she assaults the messenger who brings news of Antony's marriage. But he substitutes plenty of verbal abuse, more than in Plutarch or in Daniel's play. Jodelle's *Cléopâtre*, however calls Seleuque 'faux meudrier', 'faux traistre', 'un serf' and 'ce paillard', which may be compared with Shakespeare's 'slave . . . soulless villain . . . dog . . . rarely base'.

There are some nice touches of irony in this scene, as for example, Cleopatra's pretended abasement before the man she despises, and the way she refers to her promiscuity, of which she is never really ashamed.

After Seleucus's hurried withdrawal, Cleopatra has a curious speech (176–9) in which she seems to imply that she had to take the blame for the misdeeds of others. It is probable that the speech was suggested by some lines in Daniel's *Cleopatra*, spoken just before the Seleucus episode, when she repudiates Caesar's accusation that she had been an enemy of Rome:

> O *Caesar*, see how easie tis t'accuse
> Whom Fortune hath made faulty by their fall,
> The wretched conquered may not refuse
> The titles of reproch hee's charg'd withall.
> The conquering cause hath right, wherein thou art,
> The vanquisht still is jugde the worser part.

In any case, the false explanation of the attempt to deceive Caesar about her treasure is designed to further his belief that she has decided to go on living. In spite of Caesar's promise of friendship ('we remain your friend') and his term of mild endearment ('dear queen'), Cleopatra knows from Dolabella's warning, and from her own instincts, that he cannot be trusted.

In the rest of the play Shakespeare does all he can to raise our opinion of Cleopatra – and if this was unintentional, as some have supposed, he was uncharacteristically incompetent as a dramatist. Iras calls her 'good lady' and Dolabella calls her 'good queen' and says that his love for her 'makes religion to obey'. More significant are the love and loyalty she inspires in her 'girls', as she calls them. They are both determined to share her suicide, and it is Iras who speaks after Caesar's departure:

> Finish, good lady; the bright day is done,
> And we are for the dark.

She does not need Cleopatra's account of the shames they will suffer in Rome from 'mechanic slaves', 'saucy lictors' and burlesque actors to stiffen her resolution. Cleopatra calls Charmian noble and kind, and kisses them both farewell. They are not slaves, unwillingly sacrificed with their mistress by her tyrannical orders. Despite their obvious love of life, they go willingly to their deaths out of simple love and loyalty.

The horrors Cleopatra foresees from Caesar's triumph include sexual harassment by lictors, a satirical parody of their Alexandrian revels, and, worst of all, she would see 'some squeaking Cleopatra boy [her] greatness / I'the posture of a whore'. It has been argued that Shakespeare was here attempting, in Brechtian fashion, to *alienate* the audience by reminding them that this was only a play, not real life. Similarly it has been argued that the same method of alienation is at work when, after the assassination of Julius Caesar, one of the conspirators cries:

> How many ages hence
> Shall this our lofty scene be acted over
> In states unborn and accents yet unknown!

The scene was being played in London and in English, so that the prophecy was being fulfilled. But this was not for the purpose of shattering the illusion; quite the contrary, it was to strengthen it. In the same way Cleopatra's reference to a stage performance did not jerk the audience back from illusion to reality. It was a daring stroke to refer to a boy actor so disparagingly: Shakespeare could take the risk only because he could rely absolutely on the competence of the actor playing the part, one, perhaps, who had recently triumphed as Lady Macbeth, and probably a young man rather than a squeaking boy.

Cleopatra had already whispered to Charmian about the plan of smuggling the asps into the monument (191). For obvious reasons the audience is not let into the secret at this point: it is only after Cleopatra's death that we learn that she had made researches into easy ways to die (354).

'I am again for Cydnus' reminds the audience of Cleopatra's first meeting with Antony and of Enobarbus's description of it. She is proposing to re-enact her early love for Antony before it was shadowed by jealousy and accusations of treachery. Only after Antony's death can her love be refined and purified. The linking of her suicide with the first meeting is not made by Plutarch, and it may have been suggested by Daniel, whose heroine decked herself

> Even as she was when on thy cristall streames
> Cleare Cydnus she did shew what earth can shew.

Cleopatra tells Charmian that she can play till 'doomsday', a reference to the Judgement Day of Christian belief. The anachronism is justified by the context, for both lovers assume some kind of life after death, and Caesar, the lucky one, is threatened with the after-wrath of the gods, that is, after his death. Charmian takes up the reference to 'play' as she arranges Cleopatra's crown as a last service to her mistress.

The first Folio gives no stage direction for the exit of Iras at 231, and it is probable that Charmian should go out with her, and that both women should return, from another room in the monument, with Cleopatra's best attire, crown and regalia. 'Bring our crown and all' can be addressed to Charmian whose presence is not required in the scene with the Clown.

Cleopatra declares that she has nothing of woman left in her, that she is now constant (unlike the stereotype of women for thousands of years) and that she is no longer swayed by the inconstant moon which changes from day to day. Earlier (IV.15.72) she had said that she was 'e'en a woman'. Isis, with whom Cleopatra had been identified, and as whom she had appeared in public, was the moon goddess, and Antony had spoken of her as 'our terrene moon' (III.13.153).

The Clown who brings the asps is generally thought to provide comic relief and, it used to be thought, beneath the dignity of tragedy. Certainly his malapropisms (*immortal* for *mortal*, *falliable* for *infallible*) remind us of Dogberry's similar blunders in *Much Ado About Nothing*. These, and his absurd remark, 'Those that do die of it do seldom or never recover', will raise a smile. So also will his garrulity, his remarks on women's sexuality, and his quibbling on the word 'die'. Moreover, Cleopatra's attempts to get rid of him – she says farewell four times – would be funny in a less emotionally charged situation, and are perhaps funny anyway. Yet the general effect is not one of comic relief, though it does provide relief of a sort before the sublimity of the scene which follows. 'Clown' gives a misleading impression: he is a rustic. He shows a touching concern for the recipient of the asps, warning her four times that they are dangerous. The scene therefore reminds the audience that the approaching suicide is for real, the more necessary as it is also a superb piece of ritual and, like all ritual, a kind of theatrical performance.

Cleopatra has 'immortal longings', longings for immortality, not the immortal biting of which the Clown had spoken (although a few critics believe that her illusions are exposed by memories of the Clown's words). She has to give up sensual pleasures, such as that of wine, though not, as we shall see, sexuality. She feels a rapport with Antony's spirit; her noble act, inspired by love, having the power of reviving him in the sense of validating his love. Antony had been warned by the Soothsayer of Caesar's inordinate luck; and Cleopatra, who knew of this warning, credits Antony with mocking Caesar for his luck. As we have seen, the belief that the gods punish the lucky ones when they die implies a belief in an afterlife in which punishments and rewards would be distributed. 'Husband, I come' equally implies an afterlife. Antony did go through a marriage ceremony with Cleopatra, apparently without divorcing Octavia. Whether or not Shakespeare knew of this, the term 'husband', claimed by Cleopatra for the first time, carries the implication that by her suicide – a very Roman deed – she becomes worthy of him and joins him. She had been sarcastic previously at the expense of the married women, Fulvia and Octavia.

Human beings were thought to be composed of four elements (earth, air, fire, water) and in her reformed state Cleopatra claims that she now consists of the more spiritual elements, air and fire, elements which survive the death of the body. The Dauphin in *Henry V* (III.7), eulogizing his horse, declared that 'the dull elements of earth and water never appear in him'. So Cleopatra, bequeathing those elements to baser life, means that they will die with the death of the body, while air and fire will survive (cf. *Sonnets*, 44, 45, 146).

Iras dies first, either of grief, or more probably from the bite of the asp. This could be made clear in production. Despite the Soothsayer's prophecy that Charmian and Iras had identical fortunes, and that both will outlive Cleopatra, it proves otherwise. By comparing the stroke of death to a lover's pinch, Cleopatra is thinking of death as a lover; and Charmian later declares her mistress to be in death's possession, like Proserpine. Cleopatra's anxiety that Antony, encountering Iras in the underworld, will 'slake his passion on her' (Emrys Jones's paraphrase of 'spend that kiss') shows that Cleopatra's belief that she has become all air and fire, does not inhibit sexual feelings. The ease of Iras's death reassures Cleopatra, who had sought, as Plutarch tells us, easy ways to die; and the same idea is repeated several times in Daniel's play:

> That with one gentle touch canst free our breath ...
> That open canst with such an easy key
> The door of life ...
>   I might well perceive
> The drowsy humour in her falling brow.

The style of the death scene has an extraordinary variety. It ranges from the elaborate address to the asp, with the rare word 'intrinsicate' and its dislocated syntax:

> Come, thou mortal wretch,
> With thy sharp teeth the knot intrinsicate
> Of life at once untie

to the absolute simplicity of the line: 'As sweet as balm, as soft as air, as gentle'.

Plutarch mentions only the bites on Cleopatra's arm; but it was a common legend mentioned by George Peele in *Edward I* and by Thomas Nashe in *Christ's Teares Over Jerusalem*, who writes 'At thy breasts (as at Cleopatraes) aspisses shall be put out to nurse', that the asps were applied to the breast. Sir Thomas Browne explains the mistake by the custom 'in capital malefactors to apply them unto the breast'. Shakespeare brilliantly utilizes the legend in the lines:

> Dost thou not see my baby at my breast,
> That sucks the nurse asleep?

Charmian had addressed her mistress as 'eastern star', the star of the eastern world, or Venus. But it has been suggested that the words called up a subliminal memory of the star in the east, which led the worshippers to Bethlehem, and hence to the tableau of the Virgin Mary with the infant Jesus at her breast. 'It has also been suggested that when Charmian (I.2) wants to be married to three kings, and to 'have a child at fifty, to whom Herod of Jewry may do homage', there was another covert allusion to the Christ child and the three kings who came to worship.)

Most editors accept the emendation of *vile* or *vild* in Charmian's completion of Cleopatra's last sentence, as it consorts with her view of the worthlessness of a world without Antony, or Charmian's feeling of a world in which Caesars are successful and Antonys and Cleopatras are destroyed. Yet the Folio reading, *wild*, makes reasonable sense and satisfactory sound.

Charmian's next lines have often been used to illustrate Shakespeare's poetical mastery:

> Now boast thee, death, in thy possession lies
> A lass unparalleled. Downy windows, close;
> And golden Phoebus never be beheld
> Of eyes again so royal! Your crown's awry;
> I'll mend it, and then play . . .

The lines are welded together by a subtle use of alliteration and assonance. The idea of death as a lover and lord – which Shakespeare had used in Romeo's last speech – is followed by the daring stroke of *lass*, which reminds us of Cleopatra's essential femininity, as in her words about the baby at her breast and her reference to a maid that milks. This short colloquial word is juxtaposed with the latinate *unparalleled*, not otherwise used by Shakespeare. Its homeliness is followed by reminders that Cleopatra was also a great queen – golden, royal, crown. (Murry, in *Shakespeare*, has written eloquently on the use of *royal* throughout the play.) The reference to Phoebus, the sun, reminds us that Cleopatra had boasted that she was black with Phoebus's amorous pinches, and also that as Isis she was the moon goddess.

Cleopatra's crown becomes dislodged as she falls back on the bed. (Daniel's lines are: '. . . in her sinking down she wries / The diademe which on her head she wore'.) Charmian, having performed this last service, can now 'play' till doomsday; and she defiantly and proudly answers the question 'Is this well done?'

> It is well done, and fitting for a princess
> Descended of so many royal kings.

It is Dolabella who is first on the scene, concealing from Caesar that he had assisted in the foiling of his plans. Even the frustrated Caesar is constrained to express admiration for Cleopatra's triumph. She is 'royal' and he describes her beauty in death as 'her strong toil of grace', while he calls Charmian's action as noble. He gives orders for Cleopatra to be buried by her Antony, and the army is instructed to attend the funeral. Dolabella, the queen's last conquest, is put in charge of the arrangements.

It should be mentioned that Shakespeare has no reference to the murder of Caesarion. The omission was not to spare Caesar, but to prevent the audience from being too conscious of the price Cleopatra had to pay for her victory. For victory it appears to most readers and most audiences. Unlike Shakespeare's other tragedies, *Antony and Cleopatra* does not leave us with feelings of tragic waste – though tragic waste there is – but of satisfaction that Cleopatra has cheated Caesar of his triumph and belatedly justified her relationship with Antony.

The World of Antony and Cleopatra

6. Historical Background

Some slight knowledge of the historical background of the play is desirable; not, of course, to correct Shakespeare's 'mistakes', but in order to see what changes he made in dramatizing the events. We have to remember that modern historians often disagree with their predecessors on whom Shakespeare had to rely. He had already dramatized the earlier events in the lives of the characters who appear, or are mentioned, in *Antony and Cleopatra*. When he wrote *Julius Caesar* he used three of Plutarch's *Lives* in North's translation, those of Caesar, Brutus and Antony.

In 48 B.C. Julius Caesar had defeated Pompey the Great at the battle of Pharsalia. Pompey fled to Egypt and was there murdered. Caesar's outward grief was thought to conceal an inward relief at the elimination of his rival. Caesar met Cleopatra and had a son by her called Caesarion. (In Bernard Shaw's play, *Caesar and Cleopatra*, a love relationship is denied although Caesar brought Cleopatra to Rome as his mistress.)

In 46 and 45 B.C. Caesar defeated the followers of Pompey in Africa and Spain, and thereby ensured that his dictatorial rule would replace that of the Senate. But the Senators had their revenge. On the 15 March 44 B.C., as Caesar was preparing to leave Rome for a campaign in Parthia, he was assassinated by a conspiracy of sixty republicans (Shakespeare's conspirators are much fewer in number). Five days after the assassination, as a result of Antony's oration at the funeral, the leading conspirators were compelled to flee for their lives. Octavius, Caesar's heir, arrived in Rome in April. He is called Caesar in *Antony and Cleopatra*. From this point Shakespeare telescoped events to an even greater extent. For the next few years Antony and the much younger Octavius were struggling for the mastery, sometimes as allies, sometimes as foes. Antony besieged Decius Brutus in Mutina (Modena). Octavius offered his services to the senate and marched to relieve the town. Antony fled with his army across the Alps (as described in *Antony and Cleopatra* (I.4.57–71).

Octavius then quarrelled with the Senate and marched on Rome. Antony's soldiers in Gaul fraternized with those of Lepidus, who arranged a conference between Antony and Octavius, and this led to the formation of the Triumvirate. They began their rule with a proscription

118

– a reign of terror – the main purpose of which was the raising of money by the confiscation of the property of 2300 persons who were liquidated (see *Julius Caesar*, Act IV, scenes 1, 3).

Antony and Octavius then proceeded against Brutus and Cassius; and since Octavius was ill throughout the campaign, their victory at Philippi was largely due to Antony. Brutus and Cassius both committed suicide. Such was the conclusion of Shakespeare's earlier play.

Octavius returned to Italy and his attempts to resettle his veterans ran into opposition from existing landowners. Antony's wife, Fulvia, and his brother Lucius, without Antony's backing, fought Octavius and were defeated. Meanwhile Antony had ordered Cleopatra to meet him in Cilicia to explain her conduct during the war against Brutus and Cassius. He returned with her to Egypt as her lover, although some modern historians suggest that her motives were more political than amorous: she wanted to extend the power of Egypt.

At the treaty of Brundusium (40 B.C.) it was agreed that Octavius should rule the West, Antony the East. To cement the reconciliation, Antony married Octavia. In the following year they signed a treaty with Sextus Pompeius at Misenum, under which he retained the government of Sicily and Sardinia, and in return he agreed to supply Rome with corn. War broke out again. Agrippa, Octavius's general, destroyed Sextus's fleet. He fled to the near East and was there put to death, probably on Antony's orders. Soon afterwards, without consulting Antony, Caesar deposed Lepidus from the Triumvirate. Antony dispatched Ventidius to drive the Parthians out of Syria, which he did so successfully that he was recalled: Antony wanted to direct the campaign against Parthia in person. On the eve of the campaign, Antony married Cleopatra, perhaps because this made it easier to raise finances for the war; but the campaign in 35 B.C. proved disastrous. Octavius refused to send Antony the 20,000 reinforcements he had promised. In the spring of the following year Antony regained some prestige by conquering Armenia. He presented Cleopatra's four children with territories which could be regarded as part of the Roman empire. After that, war between Antony and Octavius was inevitable.

Antony, accompanied by Cleopatra, transported his troops to Greece. In theory Octavius was making war against Egypt. The two armies were entrenched on opposite sides of the bay at Actium. Antony's fleet was blockaded by Agrippa's and the two fleets engaged on 2 September 31 B.C. Some of Antony's ships mutinied and returned to harbour. Cleopatra, followed by Antony, broke through the blockade and sailed to Egypt, a move apparently less foolish than Shakespeare makes it out to be. Antony's troops in Greece, unwilling to fight for Egypt against Rome, surrendered to Octavius; and although Antony still had large forces, they deserted him little by little when they realized he was on the losing side.

Because of Antony's fury at the surrender of her fleet, Cleopatra sent word that she had committed suicide. This precipitated Antony's own suicide, though he would have killed himself in any case rather than fall into the hands of Octavius. Cleopatra followed suit; and afterwards Caesarion was murdered on the orders of Octavius. But Antony's children by Cleopatra were spared and brought up by Octavia, who had also acted as foster mother to his children by Fulvia.

We have to remember that the history of these times was written by supporters of Octavius. It is thought that Antony had considerable support in Rome, at least until the battle of Actium. Horace, in the ode which celebrates the defeat of the lovers, cannot withhold his admiration for Cleopatra's suicide. Virgil, dutifully praising Augustus, celebrated the victory of Actium as the conquest of barbarism and degeneracy by the more civilized West (*Aeneid* VIII). Lucan, a poet of a later generation, and one who detested emperors, deplored Julius Caesar's affair with Cleopatra, that 'lascivious fury, who was to become the bane of Rome'. By the time we get to Plutarch, all writers assumed that Antony had been ruined by his passion for Cleopatra; yet Plutarch conveys Cleopatra's fascination, and it may be that he was secretly pleased that a queen of Greek descent had frustrated the Romans by her suicide.

Notes

Chapter 1. Sources

1. See Book 1, Ode 37 in Horace, *The Complete Odes and Epodes* (Penguin, 1983).
2. Page references to T. J. B. Spencer (ed.), *Shakespeare's Plutarch* (1964). More of the wiles used by Cleopatra to keep Antony in Egypt are described in Plutarch's essay 'How a Man May Discern a Flatterer From a Friend' in P. Holland (trs.), *Morals* (1603), p. 83.
3. *Charmion*, is this well done? sayd one of them.
   Yea well, sayd she, and her that from the race
   Of so great kings discends, doth best become.
                    (Daniel)
   Yes, tis well done, and like a Queen, the last
   Of her great Race. I follow her.
                    (Dryden)
4. See J. Middleton Murry, *Shakespeare* (Cape, 1935).
5. The best account of Appian's influence is in Ernest Schanzer's Introduction to his selection, *Shakespeare's Appian* (Liverpool University Press, 1956).
6. Quotations and line references are from Geoffrey Bullough, *Narrative and Dramatic Sources of Shakespeare* (Routledge and Kegan Paul, 1964), vol. 5, pp. 76–7.
7. Nearly all these parallels were pointed out by Schanzer and Bullough; but Bullough treated Garnier as an analogue, not a source. Willard Farnham, writing before Schanzer, doubted whether Shakespeare had read it.
8. Daniel had read Jodelle's play, as Joan Rees showed, and it is probable that Shakespeare had glanced at it. The evidence for this is provided in the commentary on the Seleucus scene. Like the Cleopatra of Plutarch and Shakespeare, but unlike Daniel's, Jodelle's heroine is trying to make Caesar believe that she wants to live.
9. See J. J. M. Tobin, *Shakespeare's Favourite Novel* (University Press of America, 1984), pp. 128 ff.
10. See Gibbon's chapter in *Christopher Marlowe*, ed. B. Morris (Benn, 1968), pp. 27–46 and J. B. Steane, *Marlowe* (Cambridge University Press, 1964) for resemblances between the two plays.

Chapter 2. Construction

1. *Prefaces to Shakespeare* (Princeton University Press, 1946), I, p. 376.
2. J. Leeds Barroll, *Shakespearean Tragedy* (Folger Books, 1984)

3. Quoted in *The Critical Reception of Antony and Cleopatra* by Michael Steppart (Grüner, 1980).
4. See Revelation 8.10, 9.1, 10.6.
5. Emrys Jones, *Scenic Form in Shakespeare* (Oxford University Press, 1971).
6. Ernest Schanzer, *The Problem Plays of Shakespeare* (Routledge and Kegan Paul, 1963), p. 133.
7. John Danby, *Elizabethan and Jacobean Poets* (Faber, 1965), p. 128.

Chapter 3. Characterization

1. G. Wilson Knight, *The Imperial Theme* (Methuen, 1965).
2. Harold Fisch, *Shakespeare Survey* 23, p. 63.
3. For details see J. I. M. Stewart, *Character and Motive in Shakespeare* (Longmans, Green, 1949).
4. *Shakespeare Studies* VI, pp. 234–5.

Chapter 4. Interpretations

1. See, for example, Steven Marcus, *The Other Victorians* (Bantam, 1966) and Ronald Pearsall *The Worm in the Bud* (Macmillan, 1969).
2. Swinburne, *A Study of Shakespeare* (Chatto, 1880).
3. Maynard Mack, Introduction to *Antony and Cleopatra* (Pelican, 1969).
4. Franklin B. Dickey, *Not Wisely But Too Well* (Huntington Library, 1957).
5. *The Imperial Theme* (Oxford University Press, 1931), p. 199.
6. Ed. *Antony and Cleopatra* (Cambridge University Press, 1950), p. xxxiii.
7. *On the Design of Shakespearean Tragedy* (University of Toronto Press, 1957).
8. *Nature in Shakespearean Tragedy* (Hollis and Carter, 1955), p. 235.
9. *Shakespeare's Pagan World* (University Press of Virginia, 1973).
10. D. A. Traversi, *Shakespeare: the Roman Plays* (Stanford University Press, 1963).
11. *Some Shakespearean Themes* (Chatto, 1965).
12. Caroline Spurgeon, *Shakespeare's Imagery and What It Tells Us* (Cambridge University Press, 1935).
13. Maurice Charney, *Shakespeare's Roman Plays* (Harvard University Press, 1961).
14. *ibid.*, p. 102.
15. Walter Whiter was the first to point out the links in Shakespeare's mind between flatterers, dogs and melting sweets. He was followed, more than a century later, by Kellett and Caroline Spurgeon.
16. Kenneth Muir, *Shakespeare the Professional* (Heinemann, 1973), pp. 167 ff.
17. It may be noted that it is generally the villains or tempters in Shakespeare who repudiate belief in the influence of the stars. Cassius, tempting Brutus to assassinate Caesar, tells him that the fault 'is not in our stars, but in ourselves'. Edmund, in *King Lear*, ridicules astrology, while the sympathetic Kent

believes in it. Helena in *All's Well That Ends Well* is cautious in her estimate of the influence of the stars. She thinks they 'only doth backward pull / Our slow designs when we ourselves are dull'.

18. John Danby, *Elizabethan and Jacobean Poets* (Faber, 1964).

19. The article was first published in 1949 and bears the marks of its time, with the rivals in the cold war being almost equally distasteful to intellectuals in the leftish Christian tradition, as Danby confessedly was; and the threatened managerial revolution offered a nightmare future to us all.

20. As I am thanked in their prefaces by both John Danby and Ernest Schanzer, I should explain that Danby and I collaborated in an article on the influence of Sidney's *Arcadia* and on *King Lear* (a play I was then editing) and that I read his book in manuscript. Schanzer was a friend and colleague at Liverpool and we were co-directors of a production of another problem play, *Measure for Measure*. I was also the General Editor of the series in which *Shakespeare's Appian* appeared (see Chapter 1, note 5 above).

Chapter 5. Commentary

1. Leslie Hotson, *Shakespeare's Sonnets Dated* (1949).
2. R. Humphries (trs.), *Metamorphoses* (Indiana University Press, 1957), IX, 217–18.
3. Ethel Seaton, *R.E.S.* (1946), 219–24.
4. B. Heath, cited in *Antony and Cleopatra* (Arden edition), ed. Ridley.
5. *ibid.*
6. A. Over and M. Bell (eds.), *A Specimen of a Commentary* (1967), p. 161 ff.
7. C. Day Lewis (tr.) *The Aeneid*, VIII. 675.

Further Reading

A number of books and articles are mentioned in the notes. The following list is supplementary. Apart from the Penguin edition, to which this book is directly related, those of J. Dover Wilson (edition 1950) and M. R. Ridley (edition 1954) have been most useful.

The list which follows is in approximately chronological order.

A. C. Bradley, *Oxford Lectures on Poetry* (1904).

H. Granville-Barker, *Prefaces to Shakespeare* (1930, ed. 1946), I.367 ff.

G. Wilson Knight, *The Imperial Theme* (1931).

J. Middleton Murry, *Shakespeare* (1935).

J. I. M. Stewart, *Character and Motive in Shakespeare* (1949).

John F. Danby, *Elizabethan and Jacobean Poets* (1964) – reprinting an article of 1949.

Willard E. Farnham, *Shakespeare's Tragic Frontier* (1950).

L. C. Knights, *Some Shakespearean Themes* (1959).

Eugene M. Waith, *The Herculean Hero* (1962).

Ernest Schanzer, *The Problem Plays of Shakespeare* (1963).

Geoffrey Bullough, *Narrative and Dramatic Sources of Shakespeare*, V (1964).

Reuben A. Brower, *Hero and Saint* (1971).

Emrys Jones, *Scenic Form in Shakespeare* (1971).

Janet Adelman, *The Common Liar* (1973).

J. Leeds Barroll, *Shakespearean Tragedy* (1984).

FOR THE BEST IN PAPERBACKS, LOOK FOR THE

In every corner of the world, on every subject under the sun, Penguin represents quality and variety – the very best in publishing today.

For complete information about books available from Penguin – including Pelicans, Puffins, Peregrines and Penguin Classics – and how to order them, write to us at the appropriate address below. Please note that for copyright reasons the selection of books varies from country to country.

In the United Kingdom: For a complete list of books available from Penguin in the U.K., please write to *Dept E.P., Penguin Books Ltd, Harmondsworth, Middlesex, UB7 0DA*

In the United States: For a complete list of books available from Penguin in the U.S., please write to *Dept BA, Penguin, 299 Murray Hill Parkway, East Rutherford, New Jersey 07073*

In Canada: For a complete list of books available from Penguin in Canada, please write to *Penguin Books Canada Ltd, 2801 John Street, Markham, Ontario L3R 1B4*

In Australia: For a complete list of books available from Penguin in Australia, please write to the *Marketing Department, Penguin Books Australia Ltd, P.O. Box 257, Ringwood, Victoria 3134*

In New Zealand: For a complete list of books available from Penguin in New Zealand, please write to the *Marketing Department, Penguin Books (NZ) Ltd, Private Bag, Takapuna, Auckland 9*

In India: For a complete list of books available from Penguin, please write to *Penguin Overseas Ltd, 706 Eros Apartments, 56 Nehru Place, New Delhi, 110019*

In Holland: For a complete list of books available from Penguin in Holland, please write to *Penguin Books Nederland B.V., Postbus 195, NL–1380AD Weesp, Netherlands*

In Germany: For a complete list of books available from Penguin, please write to *Penguin Books Ltd, Friedrichstrasse 10 – 12, D–6000 Frankfurt Main 1, Federal Republic of Germany*

In Spain: For a complete list of books available from Penguin in Spain, please write to *Longman Penguin España, Calle San Nicolas 15, E–28013 Madrid, Spain*